SEARCHING FOR THE VOICE

HOW QUESTIONS LED ME HOME TO CHRIST

PAUL NATEKIN

PAUL NATEKIN

CONTENTS

Foreword — vii
Timothy Dresselhaus, MD MPH

Preface — ix
Introduction — xiii

Chapter 1 — 1
The Child Who Took Things Apart

Chapter 2 — 22
Trying on Beliefs

Chapter 3 — 44
Offended by the Answer

Chapter 4 — 67
The Cross and My Crisis

Chapter 5 — 90
Becoming Someone New

Chapter 6 — 118
A Fruitful Life at Last

Chapter 7 — 141
What I Would Tell My Younger Self

Epilogue — 164

Acknowledgments — 189
About the Author — 193

Searching for the Voice:

How Questions Led Me Home to Christ

Copyright © 2025 Paul Natekin

All rights reserved. No part of this book may be reproduced, stored in a retrieval system, or transmitted in any form or by any means without the prior written permission of the author.

Published by Paul Natekin • First Edition: 2025

Scripture quotations: ESV®, NIV® - Used by permission.

ISBN Information:

- Paperback: ISBN: 979-8-89860-983-2

- eBook: ISBN: 979-8-89860-980-1

- Audiobook: ISBN: 979-8-89860-989-4

Printed in the United States of America

Contact: www.paulnatekin.com • ipaulnate@pm.me

Bulk Sales: Special discounts available for churches and schools.

Note: Some names changed to protect privacy.

*To Gabriel, Naomi, Luca, Emry, and Ezra—
may your questions always lead you Home.*

FOREWORD
FINDING GOD'S SIGNAL IN A WORLD OF NOISE

TIMOTHY DRESSELHAUS, MD MPH

All of us are receivers, not unlike our smart phones. Our phones receive wireless signals like Wi-Fi, cellular data, or Bluetooth; they also filter out interference, or noise. So, too, we receive signals from friends, family, and the culture around us. We also receive signals from God. These signals often compete with one another and relay conflicting views of truth and morality. The urgent need is to filter out the noise to recognize the one voice that matters, the voice of Truth, the voice of God.

Paul Natekin offers a deeply personal yet broadly relevant narrative of his own journey, beginning as an inquisitive child and continuing into manhood. It is a journey accompanied by honest questions and a sincere desire to detect the authentic signal of God's voice.

Along the way, Paul addresses life's most important questions, which have significance for both time and eternity: What is truth? Who is God? Both are answered in the person of Jesus Christ, who is "the way, and the truth, and the life" (John 14:6, ESV). As Paul discovers from experience, the voice of Jesus calls to us, speaking to us through his

Word. This Word is timeless, universal, and absolute in its message.

This is the signal—the voice of Jesus—that Paul came to recognize amid the confusion and clamor of our day. When so many are distracted by false signals or despair of hearing God's voice, *Searching for the Voice: How Questions Led Me Home to Christ* is a source of both inspiration and direction.

Whether you are an unconvinced skeptic or a long-time Christian, you will be challenged by this book. For some, it may open the door to a lifelong relationship with Christ. For others, it may prompt a deeper walk with God.

For all of us, it is a reminder to start where Paul did: a child who was curious to know but also open to the truth. In fact, this child-like approach is essential—indeed required—if we are to hear and understand God's voice. "Truly, I say to you, unless you turn and become like children, you will never enter the kingdom of heaven," Jesus explains. "Whoever humbles himself like this child is the greatest in the kingdom of heaven" (Matthew 18:3-4, ESV).

This is an invitation to everyone, since we are all, like children, in great need as we stand before a great God. It is also a warning to avoid, as Paul does, the pitfalls of deconstructing the Bible. When humility is replaced by arrogance, or when God is put on trial, we interfere with the signal of His voice.

I trust you will enjoy *Searching for the Voice: How Questions Led Me Home to Christ* as much as I did, longing as I do to filter out the noise about us to hear the clear voice of God. He is speaking to you and to me. Are we listening?

Timothy Dresselhaus, MD MPH
Clinical Professor Emeritus
University of California, San Diego

PREFACE
A FATHER'S HEART AND A FRIEND'S CHALLENGE

I never intended to write this book.

For years, this story lived in scattered memories. Then everything changed.

I was six years old when I first asked life's biggest question—not in words, but with a screwdriver. Surrounded by the carefully disassembled pieces of my father's stereo, I searched desperately for the singers I heard inside. Where were they? How did they fit? What made their voices so real yet so unreachable?

That stereo became a metaphor for my life: always taking things apart, always searching for the voice behind the sound, always hungry for meaning that seemed just out of reach.

The Cultural Moment

Many in our generation face subtle deceptions infiltrating both culture and church—lies I'd wrestled with in my own journey from Soviet immigrant to American skeptic to follower of Christ. Lies about finding identity in achievement, meaning in success, worth in performance. Lies that say all paths lead to God, that truth is relative, that Christianity is just one option among many.

I've observed a cultural double standard: questioning parents' faith is often praised as intellectual maturity, while questioning secular assumptions is dismissed as narrow-mindedness. This asymmetry reveals underlying bias rather than genuine commitment to critical thinking.

A dear friend challenged me: "Your journey from skepticism to faith—that's exactly what this generation needs to hear. Not just your conclusions, but your process."

Why Your Story Matters

If you're in your teens or twenties, wrestling with questions about faith, meaning, and whether Christianity is even real—I get it. I've been where you are. The doubts that keep you up at night. The arguments that seem to prove Christianity wrong. The feeling that maybe your parents' faith is outdated.

You need more than inherited conclusions. You need to see the messy process of someone who questioned everything and came out the other side with faith intact—not blind faith, but eyes-wide-open, intellectually honest, battle-tested faith.

What This Book Is NOT

This is not a deconstruction of Christianity. My questions led me TO orthodox faith, not away from it. I maintain humble confidence in historic Christian orthodoxy, acknowledging doubts while pointing to biblical answers.

This is not a self-help manual. True transformation comes by the Holy Spirit, not self-improvement. This book emphasizes total dependence on God, not self-reliance.

This is not a collection of feel-good stories without

substance, a relativistic approach where all paths lead to God, or a promise that faith answers every question immediately.

The Urgency of Now

You live in a moment when basic Christian truths are questioned in many places. You need to know whether Christianity is actually true—not just your family's preference, but reality. Not just comfortable tradition, but truth worth living and dying for.

A Prayer and a Promise

To my children and every young person reading this—this is your inheritance. Not success strategies, but the story of how I found the meaning of life in the Person of Jesus Christ.

God is waiting to meet you personally. He's not intimidated by your doubts or offended by your questions. The One you're searching for has been searching for you far longer.

For my children, with all my love and all my hope,
Dad

"Train up a child in the way he should go; even when he is old he will not depart from it" (Proverbs 22:6, ESV).

INTRODUCTION

THE QUESTION THAT HAUNTS EVERY HUMAN HEART

What if the meaning you've been searching for isn't hidden in the machine, but calling to you through it?—the question I Googled at 2 AM after everyone else was asleep.

That childhood stereo I dismantled became a metaphor for my entire life—always searching for the voice behind the sound, always hungry for meaning that seemed just out of reach.

You might not have taken apart electronics, but you've felt the same hunger. Many people report having felt this. Surveys consistently show that the vast majority of humans across cultures experience what researchers call "spiritual longing"—that feeling that there's supposed to be more, like you're missing something essential. The Bible calls it "eternity set in the heart of man" (Ecclesiastes 3:11). C.S. Lewis called it our "inconsolable longing" or "Sehnsucht"—that mysterious yearning for something beyond this world.

It's the restless ache that whispers, "There must be more than this."

Why This Book, Why Now?

This is the story of a relentless skeptic who discovered that the meaning of life isn't something you find—it's Someone who finds you.

Born in the Soviet Union and raised in America, I grew up between two worlds. My journey took me through childhood curiosity, teenage skepticism, and young adult spiritual exhaustion. I explored Buddhism with Leo, researched Islam in high school, debated atheism with college friends, and tried to earn God's favor through religious performance.

Every path led to the same conclusion: human efforts to find ultimate meaning end in frustration. But then I discovered something that changed everything.

The Voice Behind the Speakers

While working in a recording studio years later, it finally hit me. The voices I'd searched for in that childhood stereo were never inside the machine. They were in the studio, behind the microphone. The stereo was just the delivery system.

In the same way, all of our searching—in success, relationships, achievement, even religion—isn't wrong because we're looking for meaning. It's incomplete because we're looking in the delivery systems instead of seeking the Source.

This book is the story of finding that Source. Not a philosophy or system, but a Person. Not one way among many, but THE way. Not my truth or your truth, but THE truth that stands regardless of what we think about it.

The Journey Ahead

Whether you're a skeptic demanding evidence, a believer wrestling with doubts, or a seeker somewhere in between—welcome. I was all three at different times.

The God I'll introduce you to isn't threatened by hard questions—He delights in them. The Christian faith isn't the enemy of reason; it's the foundation for it. As Peter wrote, we must "always be prepared to make a defense to anyone who asks you for a reason for the hope that is in you" (1 Peter 3:15, ESV).

This book is that defense—not with abstract arguments, but with a lived story of how faith and reason work together. You'll see the difference between religion and relationship, between knowing about God and knowing God personally.

The questions that brought you here aren't problems—they're invitations. The restlessness you feel isn't a flaw—it's evidence that you were made for more than this world offers.

The Apologetic Thread

Throughout this book, you'll encounter what theologians call "apologetics"—the intellectual defense of the Christian faith. But rather than dry arguments, you'll see how faith and reason intersect in real life:

- **Historical Evidence:** Why I've become convinced that the case for Christ's life, death, and resurrection is compelling
- **Philosophical Arguments:** How objective moral values, what scientists call cosmic fine-tuning (observations about physical constants that some interpret as evidence for design), and the necessity of a first cause point to God
- **Logical Consistency:** Why Christianity alone solves the problem of human meaning, identity, and purpose

- **Experiential Verification**: How transformed lives provide evidence for truth claims

This isn't philosophy for its own sake—it's foundation-building for life's most important decision.

The Claims We'll Examine

Let me be upfront about where this journey leads. By the end of this book, you'll have encountered these claims:

1 **God exists** and can be known personally through evidence and revelation

2 **Jesus Christ is who He claimed to be**—fully God, fully man, the only way to God

3 **The Bible is trustworthy** as God's revelation to humanity

4 **Christianity is uniquely true**—not one option among many, but THE truth

5 **Salvation is by grace alone through faith alone** in Christ alone

6 **Life's meaning is found in knowing God** personally through Jesus Christ (John 17:3)

These aren't just religious opinions—they're truth claims that can be examined through historical investigation, philosophical reasoning, and personal experience, though they ultimately require a step of faith beyond empirical proof.

What You Will Find Here

This book is:

- An honest account of one man's journey from skepticism to faith
- An integration of heart and mind, emotion and evidence

- A demonstration of how Christianity uniquely satisfies human longings
- An invitation to encounter the God who has been seeking you
- A roadmap for moving from searching to finding

The Stakes

The question of life's meaning isn't academic—it's existential. How you answer it determines how you live, what you value, where you find identity, and what happens when you die.

Jesus Himself said, "What does it profit a man to gain the whole world and forfeit his soul?" (Mark 8:36, ESV). This isn't religious manipulation—it's reality. We all live as if something is ultimately true about the nature of reality, meaning, and purpose. The question is whether what we believe actually corresponds to what is.

The Promise

If you'll join me on this journey, I promise you this: you'll encounter the most compelling Person who ever lived. You'll see evidence that stands up to scrutiny. You'll discover that faith isn't the opposite of reason but its fulfillment.

Most importantly, you'll find that the Voice you've been searching for—in success, relationships, achievement, philosophy, or religion—has been calling to you all along. Not hidden in life's "stereos," but standing behind the microphone of creation, history, and your own conscience.

How to Read This Book

Each chapter builds on the previous one, following my journey chronologically and logically. You'll find:

- **Personal stories** that make abstract concepts concrete

- **Biblical foundation** for every claim made
- **Historical and philosophical evidence** woven naturally into the narrative
- **Reflection questions** at the end of each chapter
- **Proper citations** for further study

Whether you read straight through or take time to digest each chapter, my prayer is that you'll encounter not just my story, but the God who authored it—and yours.

The search for meaning continues in the pages ahead. But I can promise you this: by the end, you'll discover that the meaning of life isn't what you've been looking for.

It's Who.

And He's ready to reveal Himself.

"This is eternal life, that they know you, the only true God, and Jesus Christ whom you have sent" (John 17:3, ESV).

1
THE CHILD WHO TOOK THINGS APART

I was around six years old—though like all early childhood memories, this recollection is likely reconstructed from fragments and family stories—when Dad brought home the stereo, a cassette player with two speakers that seemed enormous from my height. It was a Saturday afternoon, and he'd just returned from the Christian bookstore with a box full of cassette tapes: Bible stories, worship music, missionary adventures. We were a Christian family, and my father was a godly man who wanted his children to grow up surrounded by truth.

But while my siblings gathered around to listen to the stories, I was transfixed by something else entirely. The voices. They were *inside* the machine somehow. Real people—singers, storytellers, entire orchestras—had somehow gotten themselves into that wooden box. And I had to know how.

This wasn't just curiosity. This was an emergency. Those people needed to breathe, didn't they? How did they eat? Were they crying for help between songs?

The question consumed me for days. I'd press my ear

against the speaker mesh, trying to peer through the tiny holes. Were they hiding behind the fabric? Were they shrunk down somehow? At six years old, the world was still full of impossible possibilities, and this was a mystery I couldn't let go.

So one morning, while everyone else was busy, I did what any curious child with access to Dad's toolbox would do: I grabbed a screwdriver and decided to find them.

The Great Disassembly

I was methodical about it—even then. This wasn't destruction; it was *discovery*. Each screw I removed was placed carefully in a line. Each plastic panel was laid out in order on the dining room table. Whether the sensory details I recall—the smell of electronics and dust, the way the morning light caught the copper wires inside—are authentic memories or later embellishments, the drive to understand how things worked was undeniably real.

Layer by layer, I went deeper. Past the outer shell. Past the circuit boards with their mysterious green pathways. Past tangles of red and black wires that looked like the veins I'd seen in my children's encyclopedia. Surely, somewhere in this maze, I'd find the people.

But they weren't there.

I sat surrounded by the stereo's innards, genuinely confused. Where were the singers? Where was the man who told the David and Goliath story? I'd taken apart the entire world of sound, and found only silence and circuits.

That's when Dad walked in.

Two Men and a Thousand Pieces

The look on his face—I'll never forget it. Terror, amusement, and bewilderment all crashed together. His brand-new stereo lay in pieces across the table, carefully dissected by his six-year-old son.

"Paul..." he started, then stopped. Then started again. "What... what were you doing?"

"Looking for the people," I said, as if it were the most obvious thing in the world.

He stood there for a long moment, processing. Then, to my surprise, he didn't yell. Instead, he walked to the phone and called his friend—an electrician who lived a few blocks away.

"You need to see this," was all he said.

An hour later, I watched from the doorway as two grown men sat at our dining table, piecing together what I'd taken apart. They pulled up chairs like surgeons preparing for a delicate operation. Dad's friend would hold up a component, they'd consult together, then carefully place it where they thought it belonged.

"Your boy didn't break a single piece," the electrician said, shaking his head. "He just... catalogued it all."

They worked for two hours, occasionally calling me over to ask where I'd found certain parts. I stood between them, pointing, explaining my process. The electrician kept chuckling. Dad kept sighing. But there was something else in his eyes too—a recognition, maybe. A understanding that his son's mind worked differently.

Eventually, miraculously, they got it working again. When music flowed from those speakers once more, both men cheered. But I was still puzzled. The people still weren't visible. How did they get in there?

Roots in Restricted Soil

But my curiosity had deeper roots than just that American living room. It had begun years earlier, in a place where questions themselves could be dangerous.

I was in first grade—maybe second—when they marched us into the computer room at our Soviet school. This was 1991 during the collapse of the USSR—though the exact timing blurs in childhood memory, the Communist state was breathing its last—and personal computers were mythical creatures, especially in our corner of the crumbling empire. The teacher lined us up against the wall like we were about to witness something sacred, something that could change if we breathed on it wrong.

"These machines," she announced with the kind of reverence usually reserved for Lenin's portrait, "can connect to networks that reach other countries. Someday, they say, there will be a global web of information." Whether she actually used those words or my memory has colored them with knowledge I gained later, the concept was revolutionary to us.

The computers sat there like alien artifacts—bulky monitors, massive boxes, probably already outdated by Western standards but miraculous to us. I stared at them, my mind racing. How could a machine in our classroom touch another machine in, say, America? Were there invisible wires stretching across the ocean? Did the information travel through the air like radio waves?

"One day," the teacher continued, "when you're older, you'll use these to learn."

One day. Always one day in the Soviet Union. Never today.

But for me, that glimpse was enough to plant a seed. Here was technology that could transcend borders, break through the walls that kept us isolated. If a machine could connect globally, what else was possible? What other boundaries existed only in our minds?

Walking home that day through the gray concrete landscape of our neighborhood, I felt something I couldn't name. Later, I'd recognize it as the first stirring of a hunger that would drive my entire life—the hunger to reach beyond the immediate, to connect with something larger than my confined world.

Being a Christian in the Soviet Union meant being different in ways a child couldn't fully grasp but couldn't help feeling. On the streets, playing with neighborhood kids, we'd hear the nicknames. "Believers," they'd say, but not kindly. There was a sneer in it, a dismissal. We were the odd ones, the ones who chose church over state celebrations, prayer over party slogans.

I didn't understand then why believing in God made us peculiar. Everyone believed in something—the Party, the future of communism, the wisdom of collective farming. Why was our belief so threatening? Why did the neighbors look at us differently when we headed to church?

My parents never complained, never showed bitterness. They lived out their Christianity humbly but with courage —no fear, no hiding, just quiet strength. I watched them navigate a world that viewed their faith with suspicion, yet they never wavered in who they were. Their example taught me that the most valuable things are worth standing for, even when—especially when—it makes you different.

The Pattern Emerges

That stereo was just the beginning. My curiosity was like a hunger that grew with every feeding.

In Dad's garage, I found Christmas lights and car bulbs. What would happen if I stripped the wires, taped them to the bulb's ends, and plugged them directly into the wall outlet? The answer: a brilliant flash followed by a small explosion. The bulbs, designed for 12 volts, couldn't handle the 120 volts from the wall. But each failure taught me something about power, resistance, and design.

Our neighbor had a workshop where he built things—wooden toys, small engines, various contraptions. I'd slip over whenever I could, peppering him with questions. "Why does the wood need sanding?" "How does the glue know to stick?" "What makes the motor turn?" Some days he'd answer patiently. Other days he'd give me small tasks just to keep me busy and quiet.

Dad, gifted with his hands, would rebuild car engines in our driveway. I'd crouch beside him for hours, watching him diagnose problems by sound, by feel, by some sixth sense I couldn't understand. "How do you know it's the alternator?" I'd ask. "How can you tell the timing's off?"

The reactions to my questions were mixed. Some adults praised my curiosity, calling me "bright" or "gifted." Others seemed exhausted by my relentless need to understand. "Because I said so" was never enough. "That's just how it works" felt like a locked door I needed to break through.

Was curiosity good or bad? Was I supposed to simply accept things, or was I allowed to dig deeper? The mixed messages confused me, but they couldn't stop the questions from coming.

A New World of Possibilities

This hunger for understanding had traveled with me across an ocean, from the restricted world of Soviet Russia to the overwhelming abundance of America. The contrast hit me like a physical force.

In the USSR, technology was rare, precious, mostly theoretical. In America, it was everywhere—in garage sales, thrift stores, trash bins. What soviets would guard in special rooms, Americans discarded when they upgraded. The same country where I'd glimpsed those mythical computers now felt like a distant planet compared to this land of endless possibility.

The first time I walked into an American electronics store, I nearly cried. Shelves upon shelves of components, tools, kits—all available to anyone with a few dollars. No permission needed. No party membership required. Just curiosity and pocket change.

But the technology was only part of it. The real shock was the freedom—not just political freedom, but intellectual freedom. In Russia, being different meant being dangerous. We were "believers," whispered about, watched. In America, I discovered, everyone believed something different, and they announced it proudly. Bumper stickers proclaimed faith. Churches advertised on billboards. My Buddhist classmate Leo talked openly about meditation. My Jehovah's Witness friend Ivan carried his faith like a banner.

The diversity overwhelmed me. If everyone could believe whatever they wanted, how did anyone know what was true? This question would haunt me for years, but at first, I was simply intoxicated by the freedom to ask it out loud.

Learning English became another kind of exploration. The Soviet child in me expected language learning to be rigid, mechanical—memorize, repeat, perform. But American English was alive, shifting, full of slang and shortcuts.

Within six months, I was translating for my parents. Within a year, I was dreaming in English.

I realize now this was God's signature on the human mind—this ability to rewire ourselves, to build new bridges between thought and expression. Every language is a different way of seeing the world, and He gave us the capacity to see through multiple lenses. The child who dismantled stereos was now dismantling languages, finding the connections between Russian thoughts and English words.

But with freedom came a different kind of challenge. In Russia, the boundaries were clear—we believed, they didn't, we stayed quiet. In America, the cacophony of beliefs was deafening. Why did my friend believe Buddha had the answers? Why did another friend insist God was a myth? Why did some Christians shout while others whispered?

The questions that had been simple in a black-and-white Soviet world became complex in American technicolor. And I, the boy who needed to understand how everything worked, now faced the ultimate puzzle: In a world where everyone was free to believe anything, how could anyone determine what was actually true?

The FM Transmitter Experiment

By the time I was twelve, my experiments had grown more ambitious. At a yard sale, I found a small FM transmitter—the kind you'd plug into a car's cigarette lighter to play your CD player through the radio. It had a range of maybe fifteen feet. But what if I could make it reach further?

We didn't have internet at home, so research meant bike rides to Goodwill, searching through old electronics books, scribbling notes on scraps of paper. I learned about antennas, amplification, and signal propagation—though my understanding was crude at best. I discovered that different types of wires could affect radio signals, and thought that telephone lines, which ran to every house in our neighborhood, could act as a massive antenna system.

The modification took weeks of trial and error. I re-soldered connections, added a phone jack, and carefully attached it to our home's phone system. Then I invited the neighborhood kids to tune their radios to 88.1 FM.

"Can you hear it?" I called to my friend three houses down.

"Yeah. It's coming through clear!"

Five houses. Ten houses. What seemed like impressive range to my twelve-year-old mind was probably just modest signal propagation that I didn't fully understand. I felt like a pirate radio operator, though the actual technical achievement was likely far less sophisticated than it seemed at the time.

Looking back, I know how dangerous and probably illegal this was. But at the time, all I felt was the thrill of understanding—of taking something limited and expanding its reach, of solving a puzzle everyone else just accepted.

Voices from the Highway

But the FM transmitter wasn't my first venture into long-distance communication. A year earlier, I'd discovered a CB radio at a garage sale—one of those old units truckers used before cell phones took over. The seller threw in a magnetic antenna for an extra dollar, probably glad to clear out his garage.

I lugged it home on my bike, the box balanced precariously on the handlebars. In our backyard stood a small shed where Dad kept gardening tools and old paint cans. Perfect. I cleared a corner, set up the radio on a makeshift desk of plywood and cinder blocks, and ran the antenna wire through a crack in the door.

The antenna setup required what I thought was sophisticated engineering, though looking back, it was probably crude trial and error. I couldn't just stick the magnetic antenna on the shed's wooden roof, so I attached it to the metal rain gutter with wire and electrical tape. What I believed was a proper grounding system was probably just a metal rod hammered into the earth—knowledge gleaned from those Goodwill electronics books, though my understanding was likely incomplete.

The first time I powered it on and heard the static, my hands shook. Somewhere in that white noise were voices, real people broadcasting their thoughts into the ether. I turned the dial slowly, like a safe cracker listening for tumblers.

Then—a voice. Gravelly, tired, complaining about traffic on I-5.

"Breaker breaker," I said, trying to sound older than my eleven years. "This is... uh... Stereo Boy, come back."

Silence. Then: "Well, hey there, Stereo Boy. This is Big Mike southbound. You sound a little young to be running a rig."

"I'm not in a truck," I admitted. "I'm in my shed."

Big Mike laughed—a sound that came through crackling but warm. "A shed? Well, that's a first. What's a kid doing with a CB in a shed?"

"Trying to talk to people far away."

"How far you reaching from that shed, Stereo Boy?"

"I don't know. Where are you?"

"About ten miles north of you, heading to Portland with a load of lumber."

Ten miles. My voice was traveling ten miles, bouncing off the ionosphere or however CB signals worked, landing in the cab of a truck carrying actual lumber to build actual houses. The magnitude of it overwhelmed me.

Over the next months, I became a regular on channel 19. Truckers got to know Stereo Boy, the kid broadcasting from a shed. They'd tell me about their routes, their cargo, the weather in different states. One driver, passing through from Texas, described dust storms that turned the sky orange. Another, heading to Alaska, talked about northern lights dancing like "God's own light show."

These conversations fed something deeper than curiosity. Here I was, a Soviet immigrant kid in a shed in Washington, connected to a network of voices crisscrossing America. Each trucker was a window into a different life, a different perspective, yet we all shared this invisible thread of radio waves.

"Why do you do it?" I asked Big Mike one evening. He'd become a regular, checking in whenever his route brought him through.

"Do what, Stereo Boy?"

"Talk on the radio. You could just drive."

There was a pause, just static and the distant sound of his engine. "Gets lonely out here sometimes. That white line can hypnotize you, make you forget there's a world beyond your windshield. The radio reminds me I'm not alone."

Not alone. The phrase stuck with me. We were all in our separate boxes—truckers in their cabs, me in my shed—but the radio waves connected us. We couldn't see each other, might never meet, but our voices traveled through space to prove we existed to each other.

I understand now what I was really discovering in that shed. The same God who designed our minds to learn languages, who gave us curiosity to take apart stereos, also designed us for connection. We're not meant to be isolated voices broadcasting into empty static. We're meant to find each other, to know and be known.

Every "breaker breaker" was really a prayer: "Is anyone there? Can anyone hear me?" And every response was a kind of grace: "I hear you. You're not alone."

The Deeper Design

What I didn't understand then—what would take me years to grasp—was that my relentless curiosity wasn't random. It wasn't just a personality quirk or a phase I'd grow out of.

The writer of Ecclesiastes says, "He has made everything beautiful in its time. Also, He has put eternity into man's heart, yet so that he cannot find out what God has done from the beginning to the end" (Ecclesiastes 3:11, ESV). Hebrew scholars note that the word *olam*, often translated as "eternity," encompasses concepts of duration, permanence, and transcendence—a richness that resonated deeply with my searching.

That's what I was looking for in the stereo. Not just the singers, but the *source*. Not just how things worked, but *why* they worked. Every circuit I traced, every experiment I attempted, every question I asked was really the same question: What's behind all of this? What makes it all make sense?

The apostle Paul (yes, we share a name and a curiosity) wrote to the Romans: "For his invisible attributes, namely, his eternal power and divine nature, have been clearly perceived, ever since the creation of the world, in the things that have been made. So they are without excuse" (Romans 1:20, ESV).

Even as a child, taking apart stereos and blowing up light bulbs, I was reading creation like a book. The order in the chaos of wires. The design in the circuit boards. The intentionality in every connection. It all pointed to something—Someone—beyond the physical components.

The God Who Wants to Be Found

C.S. Lewis once wrote, "If I find in myself desires which nothing in this world can satisfy, the only logical explanation is that I was made for another world."[1] That's what my childhood curiosity really was—a desire that cassette tapes and circuit boards could never satisfy.

You see, God doesn't hide from us out of cruelty. He's not playing divine hide-and-seek for His own amusement. He gives us enough evidence to find Him if we really want to, but not so much that we're forced to believe against our will.

The stereo couldn't contain the singers—they existed beyond it, and their voices were transmitted through it. In the same way, creation can't contain God, but His fingerprints are all over it. The curiosity to look deeper, to ask why, to search for meaning—that's not a bug in the human operating system. It's a feature. It's the homing beacon God planted in every human heart.

You Were Made to Ask

Years later, I would learn from Hebrew lexicons that the word for "seek" (*baqash*) appears frequently throughout the Old Testament—over 200 times according to concordance studies. God repeatedly invites His people to seek Him, search for Him, ask and knock and pursue. "You will seek me and find me, when you seek me with all your heart" (Jeremiah 29:13, ESV).

That six-year-old boy dismantling a stereo was doing more than satisfying curiosity. He was responding to a divine invitation. Every question was a knock on heaven's door. Every experiment was a step closer to the Answer behind all answers.

The curiosity that drove me to take things apart would eventually lead me to the One who puts things together—including broken people like me. But that part of the story comes later.

For now, know this: if you've ever felt that restless hunger to understand, that need to know *why* and not just *what*, that suspicion that there must be more to life than what you can see and touch—you're not broken. You're not difficult. You're not too much.

You're responding to the eternity God placed in your heart.

You were made to seek.

And the One who made you? He wants to be found.

I was about to learn this the hard way—through friends who would shake my faith, nights that would test my sanity, and a moment of revelation that would change everything. But that six-year-old boy with the screwdriver? He had no idea what was coming.

Apologetics Insights & **Life Applications**

Those stereo parts on my living room floor? They were my first clue that humans are wired differently than everything else on the planet.

Why Do We Ask "Why?" (**And Why It Matters**)

Ever notice something weird about humans? We're the only creatures who take things apart just to understand them. My dog never dismantled his squeaky toy to find the squeak. Cats don't ponder why the red dot moves. But six-year-old me? I HAD to know where those voices came from.

Here's the thing: If we're just evolved animals trying to survive, why do we care about stuff that has nothing to do with survival?

Think about it:

- Why do we wonder what happens after death?
- Why do we ask if there's meaning to life?
- Why do we care about right and wrong beyond "does this help me survive?"
- Why do we look at stars and feel small instead of just seeing lights?

No other animal does this. Ever.

Your cat doesn't have an existential crisis. Your goldfish isn't pondering the meaning of life. But you? You've probably laid awake at night wondering why you exist.

That's weird. Unless...

Unless we're designed to ask these questions. Unless the questions themselves are clues.

The Bible says God "set eternity in the human heart" (Ecclesiastes 3:11). Not in a religious-y way, but as an observation: Humans are the only creatures obsessed with forever. We're the only ones who feel like we're made for something more than eating, sleeping, and reproducing.

Every kid in every culture asks the same questions:
- "Who made me?"
- "Why am I here?"
- "What happens when we die?"
- "Why is there something instead of nothing?"

You know what's even weirder? Kids ask these questions without being taught to. It's like we come pre-programmed with curiosity about the infinite.

That's either the biggest cosmic accident ever, or it's a clue about why we're here.

Kids Know Stuff Without Being Taught (That's Not Normal)

Here's a fun experiment: Show a three-year-old a watch and a rock. Ask them which one somebody made.

They'll pick the watch. Every time.

Nobody taught them this. They just know.

Show them a sandcastle and a sand pile. They know someone built the castle. Show them a book and random marks. They know the book has an author. Show them LEGO creation and LEGO spill. They instantly recognize design.

But here's where it gets interesting: Kids apply this same logic to themselves.

"Who made me?" is one of the first questions kids ask. Not "What random process produced me?" but "WHO made me?"

They instinctively know:
- Complex things don't happen by accident

Searching for the Voice

- Organized systems need organizers
- Information requires an informer
- Design requires a designer

Think about your phone. You'd never believe it assembled itself, no matter how much time you gave it. A trillion years wouldn't randomly produce your iPhone. Yet your brain is infinitely more complex than your phone.

Your DNA contains more organized information than the entire internet. Your eye makes the best camera look like a kid's toy. Your brain processes more data than all the world's computers combined.

And kids somehow know what adults try to forget: This didn't just happen.

When I carefully saved each stereo part, labeling them, organizing them, I was following a principle every kid understands: Order doesn't come from chaos. Information doesn't write itself. Voices don't generate themselves.

The Bible says God's nature is "clearly seen" through creation (Romans 1:20). Not in some mystical way, but in the obvious way a kid sees it: This stuff is way too complex to be an accident.

We spend years in school learning to ignore what we knew as children: Somebody made this. Somebody made us. And maybe, just maybe, that Somebody wants to be found.

The Voice Isn't in the Machine (And Neither Is Meaning)

I never found the singers in the stereo. You know why?

They weren't there.

The speakers carried their voices, but the singers were miles away in a studio. The stereo transmitted the music; it didn't create it.

This is exactly the mistake people make with life. They dissect the universe looking for meaning in molecules. They study brains expecting to find consciousness in chemicals. They analyze DNA hoping to discover purpose in proteins.

But meaning isn't IN the matter. It comes THROUGH it.

It's like trying to find the DJ by taking apart your radio. You can study every circuit, map every wire, understand exactly how sound waves become music, but you'll never find the person speaking. They're not in the machine.

Your brain carries your thoughts, but it doesn't create consciousness.

Your body expresses love, but it doesn't generate it.

Creation displays God's glory, but it doesn't contain Him.

The voices I searched for were real. They just weren't where I was looking.

God Actually Wants You to Ask Questions (Seriously)

Here's something that blew my mind: The Bible mentions seeking God over 200 times. Not "stop asking questions," but "seek and you will find."

Most religions say, "Don't question, just believe."

Christianity says, "Test everything" (1 Thessalonians 5:21).

Most gods hide from investigation.

The God of the Bible says, "Come, let us reason together" (Isaiah 1:18).

Why? Because truth isn't afraid of questions. It's lies that can't stand scrutiny.

My journey from stereos to radios to building transmitters wasn't random. Every question led to the next. Every discovery opened new mysteries. The seeking itself was preparing me for what I'd find.

God gave you curiosity for a reason. Those questions

that keep you up at night? That sense that there must be more? That feeling that you're made for something beyond this?

That's not a bug in your programming. That's a feature.

You're designed to seek because you're designed to find.

What This Means for You

A Note to That Curious Kid (Yeah, You):

Those weird questions you ask that make adults uncomfortable? Keep asking them.

Why is there something instead of nothing? Why do we exist? What happens after we die? Why do we feel like we're made for more?

Adults will try to give you small answers to shut down your big questions. Don't let them.

Your curiosity isn't annoying—it's sacred. You're asking the questions you were designed to ask. You're seeking the One you were made to find.

And here's a secret: The adults who tell you to stop asking? They're usually the ones who gave up seeking and don't like being reminded that the questions still matter.

To Parents of Little Question-Askers:

When your kid asks "why" for the 47th time today, remember this: They're not trying to drive you crazy. They're doing exactly what they were designed to do.

Every "why" is a glimpse of eternity in their heart.

Every "how come" is evidence they're made for more than this world.

Every impossible question is proof they're wired for the infinite.

Don't rush through these moments. Don't give throw-away answers. And please, don't say "because I said so" when they ask about ultimate things.

Instead, try: "That's an amazing question! I wonder about that too. Let's think about it together."

You're not raising robots to follow rules. You're raising seekers designed to find God.

For Adults Who've Stopped Wondering:

Remember when everything was amazing? When you'd stare at ants for hours? When you'd ask questions that made grown-ups squirm?

What happened?

Somewhere along the way, you traded wonder for wifi passwords. You stopped asking "why" and started asking "how much?" You quit seeking truth and started seeking comfort.

But that six-year-old with the screwdriver is still in there. The one who had to know how things worked. The one who sensed there was more to find.

It's not too late to start taking things apart again. Not to break them, but to understand them. Not to destroy, but to discover.

The questions you buried are still there, waiting. And so is the One who planted them in your heart.

The boy with the screwdriver was right—there were voices to be found. He just needed to discover they came from beyond the machine, calling him home.

REFLECTION

Think back to your own childhood curiosity.
What questions kept you awake at night?
What mysteries did you try to solve?
Those early wonderings weren't random—they were the first notes of a song your soul was meant to sing.
God has been calling to you since before you knew His name.

---

[1] C.S. LEWIS, *Mere Christianity* (New York: HarperCollins, 2001), 136-137.

2

TRYING ON BELIEFS

The Flower Bed Incident

Fifth grade. Fire drill. The alarm screamed through the hallways, and we filed out in practiced lines, teachers counting heads, everyone moving with that strange mix of annoyance and excitement that comes from an unexpected break in routine.

I was running with my friends—Ivan, whose quick laugh and fierce loyalty made him popular despite his family's strict Jehovah's Witness faith, and Leo, whose thoughtful nature and genuine kindness drew people to him even as his Buddhist beliefs set him apart—when I cut across the school's flower bed. Just a shortcut. Nothing malicious. I probably crushed a few petunias.

Leo grabbed my arm. Hard.

"Why are you walking on the flowers?" His face was twisted with genuine anger. "You don't know what you just killed!"

I laughed, thinking he was joking. "They're just flowers, Leo."

"You might have killed someone's grandmother!"

The other kids started laughing, but Leo wasn't smiling. He was dead serious. And that's when I realized—my Buddhist friend genuinely believed I might have just stepped on a reincarnated human soul.

That moment in the flower bed was my first real collision with a worldview completely foreign to my own. I'd grown up in a Christian home, attended church every Sunday, listened to those cassette tape Bible stories on the stereo I'd dismantled. But Christianity was just... what we did. Like brushing teeth or saying please and thank you. I'd never really considered that other people's entire reality might be built on completely different foundations.

Three Boys, Three Worlds

Ivan, Leo, and I made an unlikely trio. Three boys from different worlds, thrown together by alphabetical seating and shared lunch periods. But our differences went deeper than our last names or lunch choices.

By high school, our group had expanded. Rashid, a brilliant Muslim student from Jordan whose warmth and intellectual curiosity made him a natural addition to our philosophical lunch table, joined our conversations. Where Leo brought Buddhist meditation and Ivan brought Jehovah's Witness precision, Rashid brought Islamic devotion—praying five times daily with quiet dignity, fasting during Ramadan with remarkable discipline, speaking of Allah with a certainty and genuine faith that reminded me of my own Christian upbringing.

Ivan couldn't accept my Christmas gift. I'd saved my allowance to buy him a model car—the really cool one with working doors—and he handed it back like it was radioactive.

"My religion doesn't allow me to celebrate holidays," he said, looking genuinely sorry. "It's not personal."

But it felt personal. It felt like rejection. More than that, it felt like a wall I couldn't see until I'd run face-first into it.

Leo meditated during recess sometimes, sitting cross-legged under the oak tree while the rest of us played basketball. He talked about karma like other kids talked about baseball stats—casually, constantly, as if it were the most obvious truth in the world.

And me? I was the Christian kid who didn't really know what that meant beyond Sunday school answers and bedtime prayers. My faith was inherited, not examined. Assumed, not chosen.

But those two boys—those two friends—they changed everything.

The $15 Computer and the Quest for Answers

I started mowing lawns that summer. Not for video games or baseball cards, but for knowledge. Every Saturday, pushing that mower through the thick grass, sweat stinging my eyes, I was saving for something specific: understanding.

When the church down the street held its garage sale, I was ready. Fifteen dollars—six lawns worth of work—bought me a beige box of possibility: my first computer, complete with a dial-up modem.

While my friends were playing Need for Speed, I was typing questions into search engines that took thirty seconds to load a single page. "What do Buddhists believe about reincarnation?" "Why don't Jehovah's Witnesses celebrate birthdays?" "How many religions are there?"

The modem would screech its electronic handshake, connecting me to a world of beliefs I'd never imagined.

Hinduism with its millions of gods. Islam with its five pillars. Shinto, Taoism, Zoroastrianism—each one claiming to hold the key to life's meaning.

I'd print out pages and pages of information, my dad's printer working overtime, ink cartridges disappearing faster than he could replace them. My bedroom became a library of world religions, held together with staples and curiosity.

Battle in Biology Class

Around the same time I was exploring religions online, Dad brought home a cardboard box that would arm me for a different kind of investigation. "I thought you might find these interesting," he said, setting down what looked like a dozen VHS tapes. They weren't movies or cartoons—they were lectures by Christian scientists making the case for creation.

I devoured them. Night after night, I'd pop in another tape, watching scientists with PhDs explain irreducible complexity, the fine-tuning of universal constants, the mathematical impossibility of life arising by chance. They raised questions I'd never considered: How do you get information without an information-giver? How does non-life produce life? Why do we find design at every level of creation?

Armed with these questions, I walked into biology class like a detective entering a crime scene.

Mrs. Peterson was explaining the age of rocks, how carbon dating proved the earth was billions of years old. I raised my hand.

"Yes, Paul?"

"If different universities test the same rock and get different ages—sometimes millions of years apart—how can we trust the dating method?"

She paused, chalk hovering over the blackboard. "Well, there are variations in testing, but the general age—"

My hand went up again. "But if I was building a bridge and my measurements varied by millions, wouldn't that be a problem?"

Other students started paying attention. This wasn't my usual taking-things-apart curiosity. This was taking apart the lesson itself.

Over the next weeks, every evolution lesson became a dialogue. When she talked about transitional fossils, I asked about the Cambrian explosion. When she explained natural selection, I questioned how it could add new genetic information. I wasn't rude—I always raised my hand, always spoke respectfully. But my questions had teeth.

Finally, Mrs. Peterson asked me to stay after class.

"Paul," she said, sitting on the edge of her desk, "your questions are... challenging. And while I appreciate your curiosity, they're making it difficult to cover the required material."

"I'm just trying to understand," I said. "Shouldn't science welcome questions?"

She sighed. "Science does welcome questions. But these aren't really scientific questions, are they? They're religious."

"Why can't they be both?"

She studied me for a moment. "If you want to discuss these topics, come see me after class. But during class, I need to teach the curriculum."

So that's what I did. Two or three times a week, I'd show up after school with new questions from those VHS tapes. To her credit, Mrs. Peterson never dismissed me. But I noticed something: the more specific my questions became, the more her answers relied on consensus rather than evidence. "Most scientists agree..." became her refrain.

I wasn't trying to win debates. I was genuinely seeking truth. If evolution was true, it should withstand scrutiny. If creation was true, it should have evidence. What troubled me was how emotional the topic became. Science was supposed to be about facts, but this felt more like defending doctrine.

Those after-school conversations taught me something crucial: everyone has faith in something. Mrs. Peterson had faith in scientific consensus. I was developing faith in design. The question wasn't whether to have faith, but where to place it.

Questions at the Kitchen Table

"Dad, if Christianity is true, why don't we see miracles anymore?"

It was evening. Dad had just gotten home from the shipyard, still smelling of welding smoke and honest work. He'd been up since 4 AM, his hands scarred from years of labor, providing for our family with quiet dignity.

He looked at me across the kitchen table, this son of his who asked too many questions, who couldn't just accept things the way they were.

"I read Acts," I continued, not waiting for an answer. "The early church had healings, visions, people speaking in tongues. Where did all that go? Why is our faith so... ordinary?"

Dad's weathered hands wrapped around his coffee mug. He was tired—I could see it in the slope of his shoulders—but he never dismissed my questions.

"Paul," he said finally, "I'm praying that one day the Lord will encounter you. Not through me, not through church, but personally. When that happens, you'll understand things I can't explain with words."

It wasn't the answer I wanted. I wanted evidence, logic, a systematic theology I could diagram and dissect like that old stereo. But Dad offered something else: patience and prayer.

THE MENTOR in the Garden

Bill Shaker changed everything.

He was old—ancient to my teenage eyes—with a shock of white hair and hands that trembled slightly when he held his coffee cup. But his mind was sharp as surgical steel. He held multiple degrees, had traveled the world, could speak four languages. And he was a devout Christian.

I started doing his yard work, initially just for the money. But Bill had a way of turning weed-pulling into philosophy seminars.

"Why do you believe in God?" I challenged him one day, aggressive in that way teenage boys get when they think they've discovered something adults missed.

He smiled. "That's a great question. Why don't you read *Mere Christianity* by C.S. Lewis, then come back and we'll discuss it?"

That was Bill's way. Never giving easy answers, always pointing toward the next book, the next thinker, the next piece of the puzzle. He turned my restless questioning into disciplined inquiry.

Week after week, I'd show up with new challenges. "What about other religions?" Read Huston Smith. "What about suffering?" Read *The Problem of Pain*.

One afternoon, after I'd been particularly persistent about the exclusive claims of Christianity, Bill set down his garden shears and looked at me directly.

"Paul, I want you to remember something. Every religion in the world is humanity trying to find its way to God. But in only one religion—and I won't tell you which one—God finds His way to humanity."

The Brother Who Found Fire

While I was intellectually dissecting faith, my brother Vadim was being consumed by it.

We shared a room, so I had a front-row seat to his transformation. One night, I woke to the sound of weeping. Vadim was on his knees beside his bed, praying with an intensity I'd never seen before. His whole body shook with the force of whatever was happening inside him.

"God, I surrender everything," he kept saying. "Everything."

The next Sunday, he stood up during church service—something we never did in our conservative congregation—and took the microphone.

"Brothers and sisters, I need to repent. I've been playing church my whole life, but I didn't know Christ. Last week, He encountered me, and I'm not the same. I want to live for Him alone."

My brother—the one who used to sneak out, who argued with Dad, who seemed as spiritually indifferent as me—was suddenly on fire. He started going on mission trips, leading Bible studies, challenging everyone around him to take faith seriously.

"Paul," he'd ask me, those eyes that used to mock now burning with concern, "are you pursuing Christ? Are you telling your friends about Him?"

His transformation unsettled me more than any philosophical argument. I could debate ideas, but I couldn't debate the change in my brother. Something real had happened to him. Something I couldn't explain or dismiss.

Missionaries at the Door

My investigative method got a field test one afternoon when I heard knocking at our front door. My bedroom was right above the entrance, and through my window I could see two young men in white shirts and ties, bicycles parked on our lawn.

Mormons.

I was in the middle of researching Jehovah's Witness theology, but here was a live opportunity to explore another belief system. I bounded downstairs and opened the door.

"Good afternoon! We're missionaries from the Church of Jesus Christ of Latter-day Saints, and we'd like to share a message about—"

"Come in," I interrupted. "I have questions."

They exchanged glances, probably not used to such eager reception. Over the next hour, they laid out their beliefs: Joseph Smith's golden plates, the Book of Mormon, continuing revelation through modern prophets. I took notes like a reporter.

"How do you know Joseph Smith was a true prophet?" I asked.

The younger missionary smiled. "That's a great question. We know through personal revelation. When you pray about the Book of Mormon with a sincere heart, God will confirm its truth through the Holy Spirit."

"How exactly?"

"You'll feel a burning in your bosom," the older one explained. "A warmth that confirms the truth."

I must have looked skeptical because he quickly added, "It's not just emotion. It's spiritual confirmation."

"But what if someone has acid reflux?" I asked, genuinely curious. "Or what if a Muslim feels the same burning about the Quran? How do you distinguish between spiritual confirmation and physical sensation?"

They promised to come back the next week with answers. That gave me seven days to research.

I dove into Mormon history, theology, and apologetics. I researched their claims about Native Americans being descended from Israelites, about golden plates that conveniently disappeared, about Joseph Smith's multiple contradictory accounts of his first vision. But I also researched their counterarguments, their evidences, their testimonies.

When they returned, I was ready. Not to attack—that wasn't my goal—but to understand. How did they reconcile archaeological evidence with Book of Mormon claims? Why did Joseph Smith's translation of Egyptian papyri not match what Egyptologists found? How could there be multiple conflicting first-hand accounts of the same divine vision?

Their answers fascinated me. Not because they were convincing, but because they revealed something about the nature of faith itself. When evidence contradicted their beliefs, they retreated to subjective experience. When logic challenged their claims, they appealed to mystery. When history disagreed with their narrative, they questioned the history.

"Sometimes," the older missionary finally said, "you just have to have faith.'

But faith in what? In feelings that could be indigestion? In books that couldn't be verified? In prophets whose prophecies failed?

I thought about my brother Vadim's transformation. He

hadn't asked anyone to feel a burning in their bosom. His life change was visible, radical, undeniable. The difference between subjective feelings and objective transformation was becoming clearer.

After several weeks of visits, the missionaries stopped coming. I think they realized I wasn't a potential convert but a researcher. But those conversations taught me valuable lessons about discernment, about testing spiritual claims against reality, about the difference between emotional experiences and truth.

Years later, I would room with a Mormon at the fire academy. By then, I had a foundation for understanding his worldview, for respectful dialogue, for genuine friendship despite fundamental disagreements. Those teenage conversations with missionaries had prepared me for adult engagement with different beliefs.

The Vacuum-Shaped Hole

The quote found me in a used bookstore, tucked inside a philosophy anthology I'd bought for fifty cents:

I encountered Pascal's famous insight about human restlessness, which has been popularly paraphrased as a "God-shaped vacuum," though his actual words in the *Pensées* are more nuanced: Pascal wrote about the "infinite abyss" in humans that "can be filled only with an infinite and immutable object; in other words by God himself."[1]

Blaise Pascal—French mathematician, physicist, inventor, philosopher. A genius by any measure. And he was saying that all human searching, all our restless pursuit of meaning, stems from an emptiness only God can fill.

I thought about my successful neighbors with their perfect lawns and empty eyes. The celebrities in magazines who had everything but peace. My atheist friend who argued against God with the passion of someone trying to convince himself.

Everyone was trying to fill something. Success, money, relationships, achievement, philosophy, even religion—we were all stuffing things into this God-shaped hole, hoping something would finally fit.

The Books That Built a Bridge

Two books began to shift my perspective from skeptical observer to serious seeker.

More Than a Carpenter by Josh McDowell told the story of a skeptic who set out to disprove Christianity and ended up convinced by the evidence. McDowell had been where I was—questioning everything, demanding proof, unwilling to accept faith without facts. But his investigation into the historical evidence for Christ's resurrection, the reliability of biblical manuscripts, and the transformation of the disciples led him to an uncomfortable conclusion: Christianity's claims were actually true.

Later, I discovered *Cold-Case Christianity* by J. Warner Wallace, a cold-case homicide detective who applied his investigative skills to the Gospels. Wallace had been an atheist, trained to follow evidence wherever it led. His systematic examination of the New Testament as an eyewitness account—testing it against the same criteria used in court—brought him to faith.

These weren't emotional conversions or wishful thinking. These were intelligent men who followed evidence to its logical conclusion, even when that conclusion challenged everything they'd previously believed.

. . .

The Divine Invasion

As I researched and read, one theme kept emerging that set Christianity apart from every other religion I'd studied.

In Hinduism, humans work through cycles of reincarnation, trying to achieve moksha. In Buddhism, we follow the Eightfold Path to reach enlightenment. In Islam, we submit and follow the Five Pillars, hoping our good deeds outweigh the bad. Even in Jehovah's Witness theology, we work to earn our place in paradise.

Every religion was humanity's attempt to climb up to God, to earn divine favor, to achieve enlightenment or paradise through human effort.

But Christianity claimed something radically different: God came down.

"For God so loved the world, that he gave his only Son, that whoever believes in him should not perish but have eternal life" (John 3:16, ESV).

Not "God so demanded that the world achieve perfection." Not "God so required that humanity earn its way to heaven." But "God so loved... He gave."

The Incarnation—God becoming human in Jesus Christ—was the ultimate reversal of religious expectation. While every other faith said "Do this to reach God," Christianity said "God reached down to you."

As the apostle Paul wrote, "But God shows his love for us in that while we were still sinners, Christ died for us" (Romans 5:8, ESV).

The Stereo Revisited

I thought about that stereo from my childhood—how I'd searched for the singers inside, convinced they were hiding in the circuits. The voices were real, but they came from outside the machine. The stereo was just the conduit, the means of transmission.

Maybe that's what all these religions were—human-built machines, trying to capture and transmit the divine. Some had better reception than others. Some picked up fragments of truth. But what if Christianity wasn't just another stereo? What if it was the Singer Himself, stepping into the room?

Bill Shaker's words echoed: "Only in one religion does God find His way to mankind."

THE QUESTION Behind the Questions

My intellectual journey was revealing something deeper. Behind every philosophical inquiry, beneath every religious comparison, was a more personal question: If Christianity is true, what does that mean for me?

Josh McDowell had written something that haunted me: "You can know intellectually that Jesus is who He claims to be. But there's a deeper question—what are you going to do with this God in your personal life?"

I was approaching a crossroads. The evidence was mounting. The philosophical arguments were aligning. The testimonies—especially my brother's transformation—were undeniable. But intellectual assent isn't faith. Knowing about God isn't knowing God.

I could feel it—that vacuum Pascal described, that God-shaped hole that no amount of research or philosophy could fill. The same curiosity that drove me to dismantle stereos and modify transmitters was leading me toward something I couldn't take apart and examine. Something—Someone—I would have to encounter whole.

. . .

The Search Intensifies

As I write this chapter years later, I can see what I couldn't see then: God was pursuing me through every question, every book, every conversation. My friends' different beliefs weren't obstacles to faith—they were catalysts, forcing me to examine what I really believed and why.

The flower bed incident with Leo taught me that worldview matters—it shapes how we see everything, from insects to infinity. His genuine concern for potential suffering, even in flowers, revealed a compassionate heart even when I disagreed with his beliefs. Ivan's refusal of my gift showed me that religious conviction has real-world consequences, though his kindness in explaining helped me understand it wasn't personal rejection. Rashid's devotion to Islamic prayer showed me that faith could be more than cultural habit—it could be daily discipline lived with integrity and warmth. Bill Shaker's patient mentoring transformed my chaotic curiosity into purposeful seeking.

And my brother's radical conversion? That was God saying, "This isn't just philosophy, Paul. This is real. This changes everything."

These early explorations would shape my future in ways I couldn't imagine. Years later, rooming with a Mormon at the fire academy, I'd draw on those teenage conversations with missionaries. Debating faith with fellow firefighters, I'd remember Mrs. Peterson's biology class and the difference between evidence and consensus. Every worldview I'd investigated had become a lens through which I could better understand and articulate my own developing faith.

I was still taking things apart, still looking for the voices behind the noise. But now I was beginning to suspect that the Voice I was searching for had been calling to me all along.

The prophet Jeremiah recorded God's words: "You will seek me and find me, when you seek me with all your heart. I will be found by you, declares the Lord" (Jeremiah 29:13-14, ESV).

I didn't know it yet, but I was about to discover that the God I was investigating had been investigating me. The One I was seeking had already found me.

But first, I would have to wrestle with the most offensive truth I'd ever encountered.

Apologetics Insights & **Life Applications**

I tried on religions like clothes at the mall. Buddhism was too tight, Islam too structured, New Age too fuzzy. Only Christianity actually fit—and here's why.

The Spiritual Shopping **Mall (Everything Can't Be Right)**

Imagine walking into a mall where every store claims they sell the only real clothes, and all other stores sell illusions. That's the world religions marketplace.

They can't all be right. Here's why:

Buddhism says: "You don't really exist."

Hinduism says: "You're part of god."

Islam says: "You're Allah's servant."

Christianity says: "You're God's child."

Atheism says: "You're cosmic accident."

These aren't different paths up the same mountain. They're different mountains entirely.

As a teenager, I tested each one with three simple questions

1 **Does it make sense?** (Can't contradict itself)

2 Does it explain reality? (Why we're actually like this)
3 Can you actually live it? (Not just theory)
Here's what I found:

Buddhism: "Desire causes suffering, so stop desiring."

But wait—isn't wanting to stop desiring still a desire? And if I don't really exist (no-self teaching), who's doing all this work to reach enlightenment? It's like saying "I don't exist" and wondering who's talking.

Islam: "The Bible was God's word but got corrupted."

Okay, but if God couldn't protect his first few books, why should I trust he protected the Quran? That's like saying "God kept dropping the ball until Mohammed." Not exactly confidence-inspiring.

Mormonism: "Pray and you'll feel a burning in your chest."

I asked, "What if it's heartburn?" They didn't laugh. They said to pray harder. But if truth depends on feelings, then everyone with acid reflux has found God. That can't be right.

New Age: "You create your own reality."

Cool. I'll create a reality where I can fly. *Jumps off chair.* Nope, still subject to gravity. Turns out reality doesn't care what I believe about it.

The Difference That Changes Everything

Here's what my mentor Bill Shaker said that blew my mind:

"Every religion is about humans trying to climb up to God. Only Christianity is about God coming down to humans."

Think about that.

Buddhism: Meditate your way up (8-fold path)

Islam: Pray your way up (5 pillars)
Hinduism: Reincarnate your way up (karma ladder)
New Age: Manifest your way up (positive vibes)
Even fake Christianity: Perform your way up (be good enough)

It's all climbing. All achieving. All exhausting.

Then there's actual Christianity: God comes down.

You're drowning and every religion throws you swimming lessons.

Christianity throws you a lifeguard.

You're lost and every religion gives you a map.

Christianity sends a rescue party.

You're broke and every religion tells you to earn more.

Christianity pays your debt.

This is why the Gospel offends people. We want to earn it, deserve it, achieve it. But God says, "You can't. So I did. It's free. Take it or leave it."

"For by grace you have been saved through faith. And this is not your own doing; it is the gift of God" (Ephesians 2:8-9).

A gift. Not a reward. Not a payment. A gift.

That's either the best news ever or the most offensive thing you've heard. There's no middle ground.

Why "Follow Your Heart" Is Terrible Advice

The Mormon missionaries wanted me to pray until I felt a "burning in my bosom." That's how I'd know their religion was true.

"What if it's just the pizza I ate?" I asked.

They weren't amused.

But seriously—if truth depends on feelings, we're all in trouble:

- Muslims feel peace during prayers
- Buddhists feel transcendence meditating
- Hindus feel connected doing yoga
- That guy at the gym feels enlightened on pre-workout

They can't all be right. But they can all feel something.

Feelings are terrible truth detectors because:

1 They change (felt great yesterday, terrible today)

2 They're manipulated (music, lighting, crowd energy)

3 They contradict (two people, opposite feelings, same situation)

4 They lie (ever felt unloved while being loved?)

Christianity says "Test everything" (1 Thessalonians 5:21). Not "feel everything." Test it.

Does it match history? Does it explain reality? Does it actually work? Does it transform people? Does it make sense?

Your heart's important. But it's a terrible GPS.

Your Worldview Glasses (Why Leo Thought I Killed His Grandma)

When I accidentally stepped on flowers at Leo's house, he freaked out like I'd committed murder. Why? In his worldview, that flower might BE his grandmother.

That's when I realized: Worldview isn't just what you believe. It's the glasses through which you see everything.

Leo saw potential ancestor-murder.

I saw stepped-on plants.

Same flowers. Different glasses.

This is why "all roads lead to God" is nonsense. Different worldviews lead to completely different destinations:

- Buddhism leads to non-existence (nirvana)

- Hinduism leads to absorption into universal consciousness
- Islam leads to paradise with Allah
- Christianity leads to relationship with God
- Atheism leads to the grave

These aren't the same place with different names. They're totally different destinations. It's like saying all flights land in the same city. Tell that to someone who accidentally flew to Cleveland instead of Cancun.

What This Means for You

If Your Teen Is "Exploring Spirituality":

Don't freak out. Seriously. Take a breath.

Your kid asking questions doesn't mean they're losing faith. It might mean they're finding it. Real faith can handle real questions.

Instead of panic, try this:

- Ask what they're learning (without judgment)
- Give them the three-question test (Does it make sense? Explain reality? Actually work?)
- Share your own journey (including doubts)
- Trust truth to win (it always does)

Banning questions creates secret doubters. Engaging questions creates confident believers.

Remember: Peter denied Jesus three times and became the rock of the church. Your questioning teen might become the strongest believer you know.

If You're Spiritually Shopping:

Here's your shopping guide:

1 **Check the logic:** If it contradicts itself, it's broke. "There is no absolute truth" is an absolute truth claim. "All

paths lead to God" excludes the path that says they don't. Broken logic = broken religion.

2 Check the fit: Does it explain why you're actually like this? Why you feel guilty, seek meaning, long for love? If it doesn't explain your actual experience, it doesn't fit.

3 Check the price tag: Can you actually afford what it demands? Buddhism demands desirelessness (good luck). Islam demands perfection (five prayers, perfect life). Only Christianity says "It's already paid for."

If You're Surrounded by Different Beliefs:

Don't argue. Ask questions:

- "How does that work exactly?"
- "What happens if you fail at that?"
- "Who determines if you've done enough?"
- "What makes you confident in that?"

Questions reveal more than arguments. Let people discover the holes in their own beliefs.

Then share the plot twist: "What if God isn't waiting for you to climb up? What if He already came down?"

That's not offensive. That's revolutionary.

The teenage boy comparing worldviews discovered what Bill Shaker knew: only in Christianity does God find His way to mankind.

Reflection

What beliefs have you "tried on" in your search for meaning? Perhaps you've explored different philosophies, lifestyles, or worldviews, looking for something that fits, something that fills the vacuum.

That search isn't wrong—it's human. But have you considered that maybe the Answer has been searching for you all along?

BUT MY EXPLORATION of beliefs was about to collide with something I never expected—I was about to become offended by the very answer I'd been desperately seeking.

---

[1] BLAISE PASCAL, *Pensées*, trans. A.J. Krailsheimer (London: Penguin Books, 1995), Fragment 425.

[2] Josh McDowell, *More Than a Carpenter* (Carol Stream, IL: Tyndale House Publishers, 2009), 127.

[3] J. Warner Wallace, *Cold-Case Christianity* (Colorado Springs: David C. Cook, 2013).

3

OFFENDED BY THE ANSWER

The Night We Broke In

The theater loomed dark against the summer sky, its neon marquee advertising whatever blockbuster was playing that week. I honestly can't remember the movie—probably because I spent the entire two hours terrified we were about to be arrested.

"Come on, Paul!" My friend Jake was already halfway up the fence. "The side door's never locked."

It was a Friday night. We were sixteen, broke, and convinced that sneaking into a movie was the pinnacle of teenage rebellion. No drugs. No alcohol. Just five church kids climbing a chain-link fence to steal two hours of entertainment.

We slipped through the side entrance, hearts pounding, and scattered into the darkened theater like commandos infiltrating enemy territory. I found a seat in the back row, slouching low, certain that every patron was an undercover cop, every usher a potential witness.

For two hours, I sat there in the flickering darkness, unable to focus on the screen. All I could think about was the crime I'd committed. Theft. Trespassing. Breaking the eighth commandment. The very commandments carved in stone that hung in our church foyer.

When the credits rolled, we snuck out the way we came, dispersing into the night like guilty shadows. But I carried something with me that my friends didn't seem to feel—a weight, a burning in my chest that had nothing to do with the running.

THE DEAL I Tried to Make with God

That night, I lay in bed staring at the ceiling, waiting for the police to knock on our door. Every car that passed, every distant siren, sent my heart racing. But it wasn't really the law I was afraid of. It was something deeper, something I couldn't name yet.

I'll fix this, I thought. *I'll make it right.*

So I made a plan—a spiritual transaction, really. For the next week, I would be the perfect Christian. Double my Bible reading. Triple my prayer time. Maybe even volunteer for something at church. Surely that would balance the scales. Surely God operated on some kind of point system where good deeds could cancel out bad ones.

Monday: Read three chapters of Psalms.

Tuesday: Prayed for twenty minutes straight.

Wednesday: Helped Mom with dishes without being asked.

Thursday: Read more Scripture, prayed more prayers.

By Friday, I was exhausted but confident. Our church had a Friday night service, and I planned to sit in the front row, sing louder than everyone, and silently ask for forgiveness during the prayer time. After all, I'd been good all week. I'd earned my pardon.

But as I sat in that pew, surrounded by familiar hymns and friendly faces, the weight didn't lift. If anything, it grew heavier. The more I tried to perform my way to peace, the more I realized the futility of my efforts.

The Mission I Never Wanted

My brother Vadim had been radically transformed by Christ. Where I was still wrestling with guilt and trying to earn God's favor, he lived with an urgency that sometimes made me uncomfortable. He'd corner me with questions that cut deep: "Paul, are you leading your friends to Christ, or are you pulling them away from Christ?"

I didn't have an answer. How could I lead anyone anywhere when I was still lost myself?

That summer, Vadim signed me up for something without asking—a mission trip to Siberia as a translator for a group from Washington and Texas who did children's ministry. He couldn't go himself due to scheduling conflicts, so he volunteered me.

"They need help translating," he told me after the fact. "I signed you up because I can't go."

I was sixteen. Mission work wasn't on my radar. I agreed to go only because they needed help and my brother asked. Nothing more. I'd be a translator, not a missionary. There was a difference, I told myself.

The journey began with a flight from Seattle, sitting next to Jim, an older Christian man from Washington who would become instrumental in ways I couldn't imagine. We flew to Moscow first, then caught another flight to Siberia. It was there I first met the ex-Marine general who would lead our team.

He was older, polite on the surface, but radiated the kind

Searching for the Voice

of strict authority that terrified a sixteen-year-old. This wasn't the warm, fuzzy missionary leader I'd expected. This was a drill sergeant in civilian clothes, and I was about to enter spiritual boot camp.

Every morning: 7 AM wake-up call. Sharp. No snooze button.

Every morning: Make your bed—military corners, hospital-tight, no wrinkles. He checked. If it wasn't perfect, you remade it.

Every morning: Mandatory personal devotions before breakfast. No Bible, no food.

Every morning: Group prayer before anything else happened.

Every meal: One apple, one orange, and oatmeal. Non-negotiable.

"I don't like oatmeal," I protested that first morning.

"You'll eat it," he said, not unkindly but with zero room for argument. "If you get sick, we terminate the trip because of you, and the whole team suffers. So you eat it to stay well."

I choked down that oatmeal with resentment burning hotter than the porridge.

Our mission involved renting a river boat and traveling from village to village, hosting events in schools and public squares, bringing children's ministry to places that had never heard these stories. I was the translator, the bridge between the American team and the Siberian children whose eyes would light up at simple Bible stories, whose babushkas would weep during worship songs they somehow knew in their hearts.

But the general wasn't just concerned with ministry effectiveness. He was shaping character, and I was his most resistant project.

One afternoon, after a particularly successful event, everyone was loading back onto the boat. I stopped by a small store and bought myself an ice cream cone—a small pleasure after a hard day's work. As I approached the pier, savoring that sweet coldness, the general stood waiting.

"Did you buy ice cream for the whole crew?" he asked.

I almost laughed. "No," I said, taking another lick.

He didn't smile. "Go back to the store and buy everyone an ice cream cone."

"Why?" I protested. "It's my money. I—"

"Because you've been selfish. Maybe others wanted ice cream but didn't have time to stop. Maybe they couldn't afford it. You thought only of yourself. Go back and buy ten cones."

I stood there, my ice cream melting in the Siberian heat, anger rising in my throat. But something in his eyes—not cruelty but conviction—sent me back to that store. I bought ten ice cream cones with my own money and distributed them to a crew that hadn't asked for them.

"This guy is brutal," I thought, watching my teammates enjoy their unexpected treat. "He has no compassion."

But he was teaching me something I desperately needed to learn: discipline isn't just about personal holiness. It's about considering others above yourself.

The lessons were relentless. When I slouched into breakfast without doing my devotions, he'd send me back to my room. When I complained about the schedule, he'd remind me we were there to serve, not be served. Every correction felt like punishment, but he was performing spiritual surgery on a selfish teenager who thought he could serve God on his own terms.

One evening, after a particularly harsh correction, I lay in my narrow bunk and cried. This ex-Marine had no heart,

I thought. He was all rules and no relationship. I was there to translate, not be transformed. Why couldn't he just leave me alone?

Then crisis struck. The general became seriously ill—so ill we had to find a hospital in the middle of Siberia. I translated as Russian doctors explained he needed immediate treatment, possibly surgery. Our mission trip would have to end early.

The general left first, medically evacuated back to the States. The rest of us had to terminate the boat rental, pay early cancellation fees, and figure out how to get home. By the time Jim and I reached Moscow, we'd spent every penny on unexpected expenses.

We stood in the Moscow airport with tickets we couldn't afford to buy and less than 72 hours before our visas expired. The Christian missions in Moscow had offered to help, but Moscow traffic made it impossible for them to reach us in time.

"Paul," Jim said, with a calmness that seemed insane given our situation, "let's pray."

Right there in the middle of the airport, this man raised his hands above his head and started praying aloud. I was mortified. People were staring. I closed my eyes but kept peeking, sure security would arrest us for public disturbance.

"Lord, You know we need money for these tickets. You know we're Your servants trying to get home. Please provide."

I wanted to disappear. Who prays for money in an airport? Who lifts their hands like that in public? This was exactly the kind of emotional Christianity I was trying to avoid.

When Jim finished praying, we opened our eyes. Across

the terminal, in a coffee shop, sat a man we recognized—an American from the oil industry we'd met briefly at our Siberian hotel during preparation week. He was facing away from us, far enough that he couldn't have heard our prayer or seen our desperate situation.

"Let's go say hello," Jim suggested.

As we approached, the man turned, recognized us, and immediately reached into his pocket. Before we could even greet him properly, he pulled out an envelope and handed it to Jim.

'This is for you guys," he said. "God told me two men would come to me, and I was to give them my bonus. He said, 'These are My people, and they need help.'"

I stood there, speechless. This stranger, sitting in a Moscow airport coffee shop, claimed to have received specific direction about two missionaries he'd barely met, and had been carrying an envelope of money waiting for us to appear.

The envelope contained exactly enough to buy our tickets to New York and then to Washington State. Not a dollar more, not a dollar less.

On the flight home, I couldn't stop wrestling with what I'd experienced. Was this divine provision, remarkable coincidence, or something else entirely? The theological questions multiplied: Does God still provide miraculously in the modern era? How do we distinguish genuine spiritual direction from human impulse or emotional decision-making? What role do signs and wonders play in Christian experience?

Scripture provides framework for such questions. Jesus warned that signs and wonders, while genuine, are not the foundation of faith: "Unless you see signs and wonders you will not believe" (John 4:48, ESV). Paul taught that "we walk by faith, not by sight" (2 Corinthians 5:7, ESV), suggesting that spiritual maturity moves beyond dependence on supernatural phenomena. Yet the same Scripture records numerous accounts of divine provision—from ravens feeding Elijah to the widow's oil that multiplied.

The apostolic pattern seems to be that God sometimes provides miraculously, especially in ministry contexts, but such provision serves greater spiritual purposes than mere material need. Whether this airport encounter was supernatural intervention or natural generosity guided by spiritual sensitivity, its effect was undeniable: it challenged my mechanistic view of prayer and opened my heart to consider that perhaps God was more actively involved in human affairs than my rational skepticism had allowed.

When I got home, my mother's shock said it all. "You're making your bed? Military corners? Who are you?"

But the external discipline was just the beginning. Something deeper had shifted. I'd seen prayer work—not the desperate bargaining I'd tried after the movie theater, but real, expectant, specific prayer. I'd seen faith in action—not religious performance, but genuine trust that God hears and responds.

Years later, after I was married, I called that ex-Marine general. "Thank you," I said, my wife beside me. "Thank you for the discipline you instilled in me. I hated it then, but it shaped my life."

He laughed—the first time I'd heard him do so. "I knew you needed it, son. You had all this energy and curiosity but no channel for it. Discipline isn't punishment. It's preparation."

He was right. The discipline I learned in Siberia—reading God's Word daily, considering others above myself, praying with expectation—didn't earn me God's favor. But it prepared me to receive what He wanted to give.

I came back from that trip unchanged on the outside but restructured on the inside. I still carried my movie theater guilt. I still didn't understand grace. But now I had tools I didn't have before: discipline that created space for God to work, and evidence that He actually would.

I didn't know it then, but God was preparing me for an encounter that would change everything. The discipline I learned in Siberia—reading His Word daily, even when I didn't feel like it—would become the very channel through which He would speak. And the faith I'd seen in that Moscow airport—specific, bold, answered—would become the foundation for believing that the God who provided plane tickets could provide salvation.

The Book That Reads You

During this time, I was still researching, still reading everything I could get my hands on about faith, philosophy, and meaning. But when I opened the Bible, something different happened. Other books I read; the Bible read me.

The writer of Hebrews describes it perfectly: "For the word of God is living and active, sharper than any two-edged sword, piercing to the division of soul and of spirit, of joints and of marrow, and discerning the thoughts and intentions of the heart" (Hebrews 4:12, ESV).

I'd read philosophy that challenged my intellect. Psychology that analyzed my behavior. But Scripture did something else entirely—it exposed my heart. Not just what I did, but why I did it. Not just my actions, but my motivations.

When I read "All have sinned and fall short of the glory

of God" (Romans 3:23, ESV), it wasn't a general statement about humanity. It was about me, specifically, personally, undeniably.

When Jesus said, "Everyone who looks at a woman with lustful intent has already committed adultery with her in his heart" (Matthew 5:28, ESV), He wasn't just raising the bar—He was showing me I'd never even come close to clearing it.

THE OFFENSE of Grace

Here's what offended me most: I couldn't earn it.

Every religion I'd studied had a ladder. Steps to enlightenment. Pillars to follow. Laws to keep. Works to perform. Even my Christian upbringing, filtered through my performance-minded lens, looked like a ladder—read your Bible, say your prayers, be good, go to heaven.

But the Gospel said something scandalous: "For by grace you have been saved through faith. And this is not your own doing; it is the gift of God, not a result of works, so that no one may boast" (Ephesians 2:8-9, ESV).

A gift? That offended everything in me. I was the kid who took apart stereos to understand them. Who modified transmitters to extend their range. Who researched and studied and worked for everything. And now God was saying none of that mattered?

The rich young ruler in the Gospels felt the same offense. He'd kept all the commandments, checked all the boxes, but Jesus looked at him and said, essentially, "You're still missing the point. Let go of what you're clinging to and follow me" (Mark 10:17-22).

The Pharisees were offended too. They'd built their entire identity on being better than everyone else, on their spiritual performance. Then Jesus came along and said tax collectors and prostitutes were entering the kingdom ahead of them (Matthew 21:31, ESV).

The Broken Leg Principle

I learned something about healing when I was fifteen, flying through the skate park on my rollerblades, convinced I was invincible. The ramp was higher than usual, my speed faster, my confidence absolute. The landing was catastrophic.

Three breaks in one leg. The bone fragments had to be realigned before they could heal.

"This is going to hurt," the doctor said, his hands positioned on either side of my leg. "But if we don't set it properly now, it'll heal wrong and you'll have problems forever."

The pain was excruciating. White-hot agony as he pulled and twisted, forcing the bones back into alignment. But he was right—the temporary pain was necessary for proper healing.

That's what conviction felt like. The Holy Spirit wasn't being cruel when He showed me my sin. He was being kind. Like a doctor setting a bone, He was realigning what was broken so it could heal properly.

C.S. Lewis wrote, "God whispers to us in our pleasures, speaks in our conscience, but shouts in our pains: it is His megaphone to rouse a deaf world."[1]

The guilt over the movie theater incident wasn't punishment—it was diagnosis. The weight I felt wasn't condemnation—it was conviction. There's a difference. Condemnation pushes you down and leaves you there. Conviction lifts you up and points you toward redemption.

. . .

The Moral Law Written on Hearts

What puzzled me during my research was this: every culture, every civilization, every human society had some concept of right and wrong. The specifics varied, but the existence of morality was universal.

Where did it come from?

My atheist friends said evolution—morality helped our species survive. But that didn't explain why we often choose moral actions that hurt our survival chances. Why do people die for strangers? Why do we feel guilty for thoughts no one else knows about?

The apostle Paul (my namesake continues to haunt me) explained it in Romans: "For when Gentiles, who do not have the law, by nature do what the law requires, they are a law to themselves, even though they do not have the law. They show that the work of the law is written on their hearts, while their conscience also bears witness" (Romans 2:14-15, ESV).

We're all born with an internal moral compass because we're all made in God's image—*Imago Dei*. That's why my Buddhist friend Leo had a conscience. Why my atheist friend felt guilt. Why every human society develops concepts of justice, mercy, and love.

But here's the problem: we all violate our own moral standards. Not just God's standards—our own. We all do things we know are wrong. We all fail to do things we know are right. We're not just lawbreakers; we're hypocrites.

The Question That Changed Everything

As I continued reading testimonies of former skeptics who became believers, one question kept surfacing, sharp as a blade: "What will you do with Jesus?"

Not "What do you think about Christianity?"
Not "Can you intellectually accept these arguments?"
But "What will you do with this Person?"

Pilate faced the same question. Standing before him was Jesus—beaten, bloodied, obviously innocent. "What shall I do with Jesus who is called Christ?" Pilate asked the crowd (Matthew 27:22, ESV). It's the same question every person must answer.

You can study Him, debate Him, admire Him, even believe facts about Him. But eventually, you have to decide what to do with Him.

Josh McDowell put it bluntly: "After examining the evidence, I could no longer deny that Jesus Christ was who He claimed to be. The issue was no longer 'Can I trust the Bible?' but 'What am I going to do about it?'"[2]

The Pride Before the Fall

Looking back, I can see what I couldn't see then: my intellectual pursuit was, in part, a pride project. I wanted to master truth the way I'd mastered electronics. I wanted to dissect faith like I'd dissected that stereo. I wanted to be the one who figured it all out.

But the Gospel humbles everyone equally. The scholar and the child, the moral and the immoral, the religious and the rebellious—we all come the same way: empty-handed.

That's offensive to human pride. We want to contribute something. We want to earn our salvation, or at least assist in it. But the Gospel says we contribute nothing but the sin that makes salvation necessary.

Martin Luther, the great Reformer, understood this paradox deeply: "God receives none but those who are forsaken, restores health to none but those who are sick, gives sight to none but the blind, and life to none but the dead. He does not give saintliness to any but sinners, nor wisdom to any but fools. In short: He has mercy on none but the wretched and gives grace to none but those who are in disgrace."³

This is the scandal of grace—we must be emptied before we can be filled, broken before we can be healed, lost before we can be found.

The Performance Trap

That week after the movie theater—reading extra Bible chapters, praying longer prayers—I was doing what religious people have always done: trying to bribe God with behavior modification.

But Isaiah the prophet had already exposed the futility of this approach: "We have all become like one who is unclean, and all our righteous deeds are like a polluted garment" (Isaiah 64:6, ESV). Hebrew commentators explain that the word translated "polluted garment" refers to cloth considered ceremonially unclean—a stark comparison showing how our best efforts appear when measured against God's perfect holiness.

This wasn't just offensive; it was devastating. If my best wasn't good enough, what hope did I have?

The answer would come, but first I had to stop trying to climb a ladder that didn't exist. I had to stop trying to fix myself with spiritual duct tape. I had to admit what the conviction was trying to tell me: I wasn't just someone who did bad things. I was someone who needed to be made new.

The Vacuum Speaks

Pascal's words about the God-shaped vacuum took on new meaning. The emptiness wasn't just an absence—it was a specific shape, designed for a specific purpose. Like a lock waiting for its key, it could only be satisfied by the One who made it.

Every attempt to fill it with something else—success, relationships, knowledge, even religion—was like trying to fill a round hole with a square peg. No matter how hard you pushed, it wouldn't fit. No matter how much you achieved, the vacuum remained.

The offense of the Gospel is that it tells us we've been trying to fill the hole with the wrong things. Worse, it tells us we ARE the wrong thing—broken, bent, unable to fix ourselves.

But here's where offense becomes opportunity. Because immediately after showing us our problem, the Gospel offers the solution. Not a ladder to climb, but a hand reaching down. Not a list of things to do, but a Person to know.

The Beautiful Offense

Years later, I understand why the Gospel must offend before it can heal. You can't appreciate grace until you understand law. You can't value forgiveness until you acknowledge guilt. You can't embrace salvation until you admit you're lost.

Jesus said, "Those who are well have no need of a physician, but those who are sick. I came not to call the righteous, but sinners" (Mark 2:17, ESV).

The offense of the Gospel is actually its mercy in disguise. By showing us we can't save ourselves, it points us to the One who can. By killing our pride, it offers us life. By offending our self-righteousness, it offers us Christ's righteousness.

The movie theater incident seems trivial now—a teenage misdemeanor hardly worth mentioning. But it was the crack that let the light in. It was the first time I felt the weight of moral failure, the first time I realized that my conscience wasn't just social conditioning but something deeper, something divine.

That burning guilt was actually burning grace, cauterizing my pride, preparing me for the truth that would set me free.

Little did I know that within months, I'd be alone in my room at 8 PM on a Friday night, and three simple chapters from Genesis would detonate like a bomb in my soul. But first, I had to learn just how lost I really was.

Apologetics Insights & **Life Applications**

That burning guilt after breaking into the theater? It wasn't just teenage anxiety. It was a clue about how the universe actually works—and why we need saving.

Why We All Know Right From Wrong (Even When Nobody's Watching)

Here's something weird: I broke into an empty theater. Nobody saw me. Nobody got hurt. I didn't even watch the whole movie.

So why did I feel like I'd committed murder?

Because humans have this annoying feature called a conscience. And it doesn't care if you get caught.

Think about it:
- You lie, you feel bad (even if nobody knows)
- You help someone, you feel good (even if nobody sees)
- You cheat, something inside says "wrong" (even if you win)
- You sacrifice for others, something says "right" (even if you lose)

Where does this come from?

Option 1: Evolution

"We evolved to cooperate for survival."

Okay, but why do I feel guilty about things that don't affect survival? Why do I feel bad about lying to someone I'll never see again? Why do millionaires feel guilty about greed when they've already "won" evolution?

Option 2: Society taught you

"Culture conditions moral feelings."

But every culture has some version of "don't lie, don't steal, don't murder." Even isolated tribes who've never met each other. That's like everyone independently inventing the exact same iPhone. Suspicious.

Option 3: There's actual right and wrong

"Moral law is real, like gravity is real."

This explains why:
- We feel guilty even when alone
- We judge others by standards we didn't invent
- We say things like "that's not fair!" expecting others to agree
- We know the difference between what IS and what OUGHT to be

The Bible says God's law is "written on our hearts" (Romans 2:14-15). Not in our heads (that's learned). On our hearts (that's built-in).

My theater guilt wasn't mental illness. It was my internal moral GPS saying, "Wrong way, buddy."

Why Being "Good" Never Works (Trust Me, I Tried)

After the theater break-in, I went into spiritual overdrive:

- Read the Bible for hours (fell asleep drooling on Leviticus)
- Prayed until my knees hurt (mostly begging God not to be mad)
- Was extra nice to everyone (they thought I was dying)
- Didn't sin for a whole week (unless you count pride about not sinning)

Guess what? Still felt guilty.

Here's why trying harder always fails:

Problem #1: How good is good enough?

51%? 75%? 99.9%?

If God grades on a curve, what's the curve?

If it's pass/fail, what's passing?

Nobody knows. That's terrifying.

Problem #2: Your motives are trash

Even when you do good things, why do you really do them?

- To feel better about yourself
- To impress someone
- To earn God points
- To avoid hell

That's not pure goodness. That's self-interest dressed up nice.

Problem #3: You can't undo the past

If I murder someone then volunteer at 100 orphanages, is the person less dead?

If I lie then tell 1,000 truths, did the lie disappear?

Good deeds don't erase bad deeds. They just sit next to them.

Problem #4: The problem is inside

Jesus said if you hate someone, you're a murderer at heart.

If you lust, you're an adulterer at heart.

The problem isn't just what you DO. It's what you ARE.

Every religion says "Try harder!"

- Buddhism: Follow the 8-fold path perfectly
- Islam: Five pillars, perfect submission
- Hinduism: Work off your karma for who knows how many lives
- Even fake Christianity: Be good enough for God

Only real Christianity says: "You can't do it. So I did it for you."

That's either offensive or beautiful. Depends if you're still trying to save yourself.

Why Truth Has to Hurt First (The Broken Bone Principle)

Ever had a broken bone set? The doctor has to hurt you to heal you. They can't just pat your arm and say "Feel better!" They have to:

1 Show you it's broken (x-ray of reality)
2 Reset the bone (painful but necessary)
3 Let it heal properly (time and patience)

The Gospel works the same way.

It has to tell you you're broken before it can fix you.

It has to kill your pride before it can give you life.

It has to show you you're lost before it can save you.

This is why the Gospel offends people:

- "You're saying I'm not good enough?" (Correct)
- "You're saying I can't save myself?" (Exactly)
- "You're saying I need help?" (Bingo)

Nobody likes hearing that. But it's the only honest diagnosis.

Jesus said, "Those who are well have no need of a physician, but those who are sick" (Mark 2:17).

The Gospel isn't for people who think they're fine.

It's for people who know they're not.

That Guilt You Feel? It's Not God Hating You

Here's what I wish someone had told teenage me:

That burning guilt isn't God being angry. It's God calling you home.

Think about it:

- If God hated you, why would He bother convicting you?
- If He didn't care, why would your conscience work?
- If He wanted to destroy you, why give you a chance to turn around?

Guilt is God's alarm system. It's not saying "I hate you." It's saying "You're going the wrong way. Turn around. Come home."

The intensity of the guilt matches the intensity of His love. He's not casual about you. He's passionate about you. The conviction that feels like condemnation is actually invitation.

Without conviction, we'd never know we need saving.

Without guilt, we'd never seek grace.

Without offense, we'd never surrender.

The thing that feels like judgment is actually mercy in disguise.

Three Stories of Truth That Hurt Before It Healed

Sarah's Story: The Straight-A Student

Sarah had it all together. 4.0 GPA, volunteer work, never missed church. She was the "good kid" everyone pointed to. But inside, she was exhausted from performing.

Then someone told her: "You know all that achieving? God's not impressed. He loves you the same at your worst as at your best."

It offended her. It hurt. It made her angry. All that work for nothing?

But then... relief. She could stop performing. She could just be loved. She could fail and still be accepted. The truth that wounded her pride healed her soul.

Marcus's Story: The Rebel

Marcus was the opposite. Drugs, parties, petty crime. He wore his rebellion like armor. "God could never love someone like me," he'd say.

Then someone told him: "You're right. You can't earn God's love. Good news—you don't have to. It's free."

It offended him. Why should he get the same grace as "good" people? Where's the justice in that?

But then he realized: If he couldn't earn it, he couldn't lose it. If it wasn't based on performance, his failures couldn't disqualify him. The scandal of grace became his salvation.

Jennifer's Story: The Religious Girl

Jennifer grew up in church. Knew all the verses.

Followed all the rules. Thought she was saved because she was good.

Then someone asked her: "If being good saves you, why did Jesus have to die?"

It shattered her. Twenty years of religion crumbled. She wasn't saved—she was just religious.

But from those ruins came real faith. Not in her goodness but in His. Not in her performance but in His sacrifice. The demolition of her religion was the beginning of her relationship.

Your Story:

What offends you about the Gospel?
- That you're not good enough? (Join the club)
- That you need saving? (Welcome to humanity)
- That it's free? (That's the whole point)

The very thing that offends you might be the truth that sets you free.

The wound comes before the healing.

The offense comes before the grace.

The breaking comes before the breakthrough.

That's not cruel. That's necessary. You can't fix what you won't admit is broken.

The teenager burning with guilt over a petty theft was experiencing the beautiful offense of the Gospel—truth that wounds before it heals, conviction that points to grace.

Reflection

What offends you about the Gospel?

Is it the claim that you can't earn God's favor?

The idea that your best efforts aren't enough?

The scandal of grace given freely to those who don't deserve it?

That offense might be the very thing God is using to prepare your heart for the truth that will transform your life.

---

[1] C.S. LEWIS, *The Problem of Pain* (New York: HarperOne, 2001), 91.

[2] Josh McDowell, *More Than a Carpenter* (Carol Stream, IL: Tyndale House Publishers, 2009), 13.

[3] Martin Luther, *Commentary on Romans*, trans. J. Theodore Mueller (Grand Rapids: Kregel Publications, 1954; originally written 1515-1516), 25.

4

THE CROSS AND MY CRISIS

The Businessman's Bargain

The coffee shop hummed with the usual morning chaos—espresso machines hissing, milk steamers screaming, conversations blending into white noise. But across from me sat a man whose words cut through it all like a blade.

"Paul, I want to make you a deal."

His name was Michael. Mid-forties, successful, owner of two companies—one in IT, one in networking. I'd started doing some electrical work for him, fixing his office wiring, setting up his systems. But our conversations had quickly moved beyond business.

He pulled out a piece of paper and began writing.

"I'm serious about this," he said, his pen moving across the page. "I'll give you one of my companies. Sign it over completely. In exchange, you give me what you have."

I laughed nervously. "What do I have? I'm eighteen. I fix computers and pull cable."

"You have hunger," he said, looking up at me with eyes

that held a strange desperation. "You have that fire, that search for meaning. I had it once. I want it back."

He slid the paper across the table. It was an actual contract.

The Man Who Had Everything

Michael's story unfolded over several coffee meetings, each detail more sobering than the last.

"I grew up like you," he said. "Christian family. Genuine faith as a young man. But then I looked around at my peers—the non-Christians—and they were succeeding. Nice cars, big houses, beautiful wives. They had everything, and they didn't need God for any of it."

He stirred his coffee absently, lost in memory.

"So I made a deal with God. I actually said it out loud: 'God, I'm putting you on hold. Let me build my empire first. Once I'm successful, once I have what they have, I'll come back to you. I'll dedicate my life to you then.'"

The plan worked—at least the first part. Michael built not one but two successful companies. He married a beautiful woman. They had two kids. The American dream, fully realized.

"But Paul," he said, his voice dropping, "I gained everything and lost everything. My wife left me—said I'd become someone she didn't recognize. My kids won't talk to me. They see me as a walking ATM, nothing more. And that hunger for God? That fire I once had? It's gone. I can't find it again."

He looked at the contract still sitting between us.

"I know exactly who I need to pursue. I know it's God. But the hunger is dead. I'd trade everything I've built to have what you have—that desperate need to know Him."

The Question That Haunted

My brother Vadim was on another mission trip, but his words echoed in his absence: "Paul, are you bringing your friends to Christ, or are you pulling them away?"

It was Friday night. My friends were heading to the bowling alley—our usual weekend routine. Basketball, skating, bowling, repeat. Good kids doing good kid things, but Christ was never part of the equation.

"Come on, Paul!" Dima called from his car. "We've got a lane reserved!"

"I can't tonight," I heard myself saying. "I need to figure something out."

They tried to convince me, but something in my voice must have told them this was different. They drove off, leaving me alone with a decision I couldn't articulate yet.

8 PM. My room. Alone.

The house was quiet. Parents asleep. Vadim still overseas. Just me and this overwhelming sense that something was about to change.

The Store Receipt

But before I tell you about that night, I need to tell you about my father and a receipt.

We were at the hardware store—Dad and I. Being immigrants from the Soviet Union, Dad's English was functional but limited, so I often came along as translator. We were buying tools for a project, nothing expensive, just the usual supplies.

At the checkout, the cashier scanned our items, chatting cheerfully as she worked. But she missed one—a small tool, maybe worth five dollars. She dropped it in the bag without scanning it.

I noticed. Dad noticed. The cashier didn't.

We were almost to the car when Dad stopped.

"Paul, tell her we didn't pay for this." He held up the tool.

"Dad, it's five dollars. It's her mistake. The store won't even notice."

His face changed—not angry, but deeply serious. "Paul, this is not about the store. This is about who we are. We are children of God. We do what's right because that's who we are, not because someone is watching."

We walked back. I translated as Dad explained the mistake. The cashier was shocked—not by the error, but by the honesty. "Most people would have just kept it," she said.

"We're not most people," Dad replied in his broken English. "We are God's people."

That moment preached louder than any sermon. My father wasn't trying to earn God's favor through good deeds. He was living out an identity—Christ's identity expressed through him.

THE MORNING PRAYER Warrior

Every morning at 4 AM, before heading to his welding job at the shipyard, Dad would quietly slip into our rooms. I knew because I would feel the slight creak of the floorboards and hear his gentle whispers as he prayed beside our beds.

He'd pray for each of us by name.

"Lord, I pray for Edward. Strengthen him as the oldest. Help him lead his brothers and sisters well."

"I pray for Sergey. Give him wisdom. Guide his steps."

"I pray for Vadim. Keep the fire burning in him. Use him for your kingdom."

"I pray for Paul. Draw him to yourself. Don't let him go. Whatever it takes, bring him to you."

"I pray for Svetlana. Protect her heart. Let her know how precious she is to you."

"I pray for Shana. Cover her with your grace. May she always walk in your light."

Every morning. Every single morning. While the world slept, my father stood in the gap for his children.

I'd lie there in the darkness, pretending to sleep, listening to this man who worked with his scarred hands all day petition the God of the universe for his sons' and daughters' souls. He never knew I was listening. He never did it for show. This was simply who he was—a man who knew God personally and believed prayer changed things.

God Doesn't Have Grandchildren

"God doesn't have grandchildren, only children."

I'd heard this phrase my whole life, but suddenly it landed like a punch. If God doesn't have grandchildren, then my parents' faith wasn't enough. My brothers' conversions didn't cover me. I couldn't inherit this. I couldn't ride anyone else's coattails into the kingdom.

The apostle John had written it clearly: "But to all who did receive him, who believed in his name, he gave the right to become children of God, who were born, not of blood nor of the will of the flesh nor of the will of man, but of God" (John 1:12-13, ESV).

Not of blood—not through family lineage.

Not of the will of the flesh—not through human effort.

Not of the will of man—not through someone else's decision.

But of God.

This was personal. Individual. Between me and God alone.

The Night Everything Changed

8 PM became 9 PM. I sat on my bed, restless, agitated, feeling like something was building inside me that I couldn't name.

Then came the thought—no, stronger than a thought. An impression, pressing on my mind with unusual clarity:

Read Genesis 1, 2, and 3.

I almost laughed. Genesis? The creation account? I'd read it dozens of times in Sunday school. Adam, Eve, garden, snake, apple—I knew the story.

Read it.

The impression grew stronger, almost unbearable. I grabbed my Bible, worn from years of dutiful but disconnected reading, and opened to the beginning.

"In the beginning, God created the heavens and the earth" (Genesis 1:1, ESV).

I'd read these words before. But this time... this time was different.

When Pages Speak

I didn't hear an audible voice. There was no angelic vision, no supernatural manifestation. But as I read those familiar words, they became alive in a way I can barely describe.

"Then God said, 'Let there be light,' and there was light" (Genesis 1:3, ESV).

God spoke, and reality obeyed. A word from His mouth, and photons burst into existence.

"And God said, 'Let the waters swarm with swarms of living creatures'" (Genesis 1:20, ESV).

"And God said, 'Let the earth bring forth living creatures'" (Genesis 1:24, ESV).

Everything—spoken into existence. The power of the Word creating ex nihilo, out of nothing.

But then I reached Genesis 2:7, and everything shifted:

"Then the Lord God formed the man of dust from the ground and breathed into his nostrils the breath of life, and the man became a living creature."

The Heart Finds Its Home

What happened next is difficult to describe. It wasn't just intellectual understanding—something deeper shifted inside me. As I sat there in my room, those ancient words penetrating places I didn't know existed, I felt my heart... settle. Like a restless child finally finding their parent's arms. Like a ship that had been circling in fog suddenly spotting the lighthouse.

My heart found its home.

All my life, I'd felt this restlessness, this sense of being slightly out of place even in familiar surroundings. The constant taking apart of things, the endless questions, the research into different religions—it was all a search for home, for the place where my soul could finally exhale and say, "This is where I belong."

And there, reading about God forming man with His own hands, breathing His own breath into dust, I understood. The restlessness wasn't a defect. It was homesickness. I'd been longing for the One who made me, searching for the breath that first filled my lungs in Eden.

Tears were flowing freely now, but they weren't tears

of sadness. They were tears of recognition. Like the moment when adopted children finally meet their birth parents and see their own eyes looking back at them. I was seeing where I came from, who I belonged to, why I existed.

"Almost like my heart understood the meaning behind those voices," I would later tell people. Those voices I'd searched for in the stereo, the ones I'd tried to track down through circuits and speakers—they weren't hiding. They were calling. And they weren't random signals from distant stations. They were the voice of my Father, speaking through creation, through conscience, through His Word, saying, "Come home."

The Difference That Changes Everything

Formed. Not spoken. Formed.

It was as if God was speaking directly to my searching heart:

Paul, do you see? When I created light, I spoke. When I created stars, I spoke. When I filled the seas with life, I spoke. But when it came to humanity—when it came to you—I didn't just speak.

I formed. With my hands. Like a potter with clay, like an artist with his masterpiece. You weren't mass-produced. You weren't an afterthought. You were crafted, shaped, personally designed.

And then—Paul, pay attention—I breathed. My breath. My life. Into you.

It suddenly made perfect sense. That emptiness in every human heart? It's there because God's own breath is what animated us. We're not just physical beings who developed spiritual awareness. We're spiritual beings, animated by the breath of God Himself, temporarily housed in physical bodies.

The Garden Walk

I kept reading, and Genesis 3:8 stopped me cold:

"And they heard the sound of the Lord God walking in the garden in the cool of the day."

God walked with them. Not observed from a distance. Not communicated through intermediaries. He walked with them in the cool of the day—that perfect evening hour when work is done and friendship flourishes.

This wasn't a God who created and abandoned. This was a God who created for relationship.

That's what you've been searching for, Paul. Not rules. Not religion. Not intellectual answers. Relationship. I created you for fellowship with Me. That emptiness you feel? It's homesickness for Eden, for the walks we were meant to take together.

The Identity Crisis Resolved

Tears were streaming down my face, though I hadn't noticed when they started. Everything clicked into place:

- Why the stereo couldn't satisfy my curiosity (I was looking for the Singer, not just the song)
- Why different religions felt incomplete (they were humanity reaching for God, not God reaching for humanity)
- Why success hadn't satisfied Michael (he was trying to fill a God-shaped void with God-substitutes)
- Why my father's integrity mattered (his identity was hidden in Christ)
- Why conviction felt so heavy (I was living outside my created purpose)

"So God created man in his own image, in the image of God he created him; male and female he created them" (Genesis 1:27, ESV).

Imago Dei. The image of God. That's why I could reason, create, love, choose. That's why I longed for meaning, purpose, eternity. I was made in the image of an eternal, purposeful, meaningful God.

The Prayer in the Closet

The next day, I couldn't wait to get home from school. I ran into the house, grabbed a chair, and did something that must have looked insane to anyone watching—I went into my closet and closed the door.

Jesus had said, "But when you pray, go into your room and shut the door and pray to your Father who is in secret" (Matthew 6:6, ESV).

I took it literally.

Sitting in the darkness among hanging clothes and stored boxes, I talked to God for the first time—really talked, not recited or performed or pretended.

"God, it's Paul. I know you know that, but I need to say it. I'm Paul, the one you formed, the one you breathed life into. I want to know you. Not know about you—know YOU. I want those walks in the garden. I want what we were meant to have before everything broke."

"I don't know how to do this. I don't know what comes next. But that emptiness inside me—I feel it. That breath you breathed—I need it renewed. I'm not trying to earn anything anymore. I'm just... here. Your child, not your grandchild. Yours."

. . .

The Beginning of Everything

C.S. Lewis once wrote in his essay 'Is Theology Poetry?': "I believe in Christianity as I believe that the Sun has risen, not only because I see it, but because by it I see everything else."[1]

That night with Genesis, that prayer in the closet—it wasn't the end of my searching. It was the beginning of my finding. Or rather, it was the moment I realized I'd been found all along.

The conviction that had offended me was actually God calling me home.

The questions that had driven me were actually God drawing me to Himself.

The emptiness I'd felt was actually space He'd reserved for Himself.

My identity wasn't in what I achieved or knew or did. It wasn't even in what I believed. It was in whose I was—formed by God, breathed into by God, made for God.

The crisis was over. The Cross had won. Not because I'd figured it all out, but because I'd finally stopped trying to.

A Testimony Born in Peru

Years later, I would understand just how universal this Genesis revelation was. On a mission trip to Peru, I found myself sitting across from a university professor who had invited me specifically to discuss Christianity. He was brilliant—the kind of intellect that made you choose your words carefully. But beneath his academic exterior, I sensed a familiar restlessness.

We talked for an hour about theology, philosophy, evidence for faith. I shared my testimony, but partway through, I stopped. Something prompted me to ask a different question.

"Professor, may I ask you something?"

"Of course."

"What do you do when you come home from work? When you have money in your bank account, when everything is well with your family, but something within you—there's a void. There's almost like a hollow emptiness that's calling out for something greater."

His coffee cup paused halfway to his lips. His eyes widened slightly.

"You don't have to answer," I continued. "But often what we do as humans, we try to fill that void with something. Somebody turns on the TV, somebody turns on music, somebody brings wine to the table to cheer themselves up. We do anything to silence that voice, to avoid those thoughts that whisper, 'Hey, there's something more to life.'"

The professor set down his cup. For a moment, he just stared at me.

"How did you know?" he finally asked. "That's exactly what I've been wrestling with. Everything looks good from the outside. I have tenure, a good salary, a loving family. But you're right—there's this... emptiness. This voice I keep trying to silence."

I smiled, remembering my own journey. "That void has a shape, Professor. It's God-shaped. And it can only be filled by the One who created it."

Then I told him about Genesis. About God forming man with His hands, breathing His own life into us. About how that divine breath created a vacuum that pulls us back to our source. About how every human restlessness is actually homesickness for Eden.

"You see," I explained, "that void you feel? It's not a flaw.

It's a feature. God built it into you so you'd never be satisfied with anything less than Him. Every attempt to fill it with success, pleasure, or distraction is like trying to breathe underwater. You're using the wrong element."

The professor leaned forward. "So what happened to you? How did you fill this void?"

"I didn't fill it,' I said. "I let Him fill it. The same God who breathed life into Adam breathed new life into me. And that restlessness? It finally went quiet. Not because I found all the answers, but because I found the One who is the answer."

By the end of our conversation, this brilliant professor was weeping. "I've spent my whole career studying human nature," he said, "but you've just explained something about myself I could never understand. That void—I've been running from it my whole life."

"Stop running," I told him. "Turn around. He's been pursuing you all along."

That testimony tool—the spiritual emptiness revealed in Genesis—would become one of the most powerful ways I'd share the Gospel. Because everyone, from Peruvian professors to American executives, from teenagers to seniors, knows that void. They feel it in quiet moments, in success that doesn't satisfy, in achievements that leave them empty.

And Genesis explains why.

The Discipline of the Secret Place

After that Genesis encounter, after my heart found its home, something practical had to change. I couldn't go back to casual Christianity, to inherited faith, to secondhand relationship with God. I needed to cultivate what I'd discovered.

The prayer closet became my discipline.

Every day after school, I'd grab a chair, enter my bedroom closet, and shut the door. It sounds extreme, maybe even silly. But Jesus had said, "When you pray, go into your room and shut the door and pray to your Father who is in secret" (Matthew 6:6, ESV). I took it literally.

In that cramped space, surrounded by hanging clothes and the smell of leather shoes, I learned to talk to God. Not perform prayers. Not recite religious phrases. Just... talk. Like He was really there. Because He was.

"God, it's Paul again. I know You know that, but I need to say it. I'm here. Your kid. The one You formed, the one You breathed life into."

Some days I'd bring my Bible, reading by the thin line of light under the door. Other days I'd just sit in the darkness and pour out my heart. Questions, fears, dreams, confusion—it all came out in that closet.

What amazed me was how this routine transformed from duty to delight. At first, I forced myself to maintain the discipline. But soon, I found myself looking forward to it. The closet became my secret place, my daily appointment with the One who'd revealed Himself in Genesis.

I realize now that the discipline instilled by that ex-Marine general in Siberia had prepared me for this. He'd taught me consistency when I didn't feel like it. He'd shown me that character is built in routine, not in occasional bursts of enthusiasm.

"Discipline isn't punishment," he'd said. "It's preparation."

He was right. The discipline of making my bed with military corners had prepared me for the discipline of daily prayer. The structure of morning devotions in Siberia had created a framework for personal encounter with God.

In that closet, I discovered what Brother Lawrence, a

Searching for the Voice

Carmelite monk, called "practicing the presence of God"—maintaining awareness of God's presence throughout daily life. It wasn't about the location—God wasn't more present in closets than anywhere else. It was about the focus. In that small, dark space, with no distractions, no performance pressure, no one to impress, I could simply be with Him.

The transformation was gradual but undeniable. The young man who entered that closet angry and confused began to emerge peaceful and purposeful. The questions didn't all get answered, but they stopped tormenting me. The void inside me wasn't just acknowledged—it was being filled, day by day, prayer by prayer.

My family noticed the change. "Paul's different," I overheard my mother tell my father. "He's... settled. Like he's found what he was looking for."

She was right. In that closet, talking to the God who formed me, breathing in the presence of the One who first breathed into me, I'd found what every human heart searches for: home.

The discipline became so regular that missing a day felt like missing a meal. Not because God would punish me, but because I'd miss Him. The relationship that began with Genesis revelation was deepening through daily conversation.

Years later, I would understand what the Psalmist meant: "As a deer pants for flowing streams, so pants my soul for you, O God" (Psalm 42:1, ESV). The thirst was real. The satisfaction was real. And it all started with a chair in a closet and a teenager finally talking to his true Father.

Now came the hard part.

Apologetics Insights & Life Applications

When I opened Genesis to prove it wrong, something weird happened. It read me instead. And Michael's million-dollar offer proved something even weirder—success without God is worthless.

The Millionaire Who'd Trade Everything (And What It Proves)

Michael had everything: Multiple businesses. Big house. Trophy life.

Then he heard about my spiritual experience and literally offered to trade it all for what I had. Not joking. Dead serious. A millionaire wanting to swap places with a broke teenager.

That's insane. Unless...

Unless there's something more valuable than money.

Unless success doesn't equal satisfaction.

Unless we're made for more than material things.

Think about this pattern:

- Robin Williams: Rich, famous, beloved. Died empty.
- Anthony Bourdain: Dream job, traveled the world. Still not enough.
- Every lottery winner who ends up miserable.
- Every celebrity in rehab.
- Every billionaire still working 80-hour weeks. (If money satisfied, why not stop?)

Here's the thing: If we're just evolved animals, getting food, shelter, and mates should make us happy. That's what makes animals happy. My dog doesn't have existential crises after eating.

But humans? We achieve everything and feel... nothing.

We're the only creatures who can have everything and still feel empty.

We're the only ones who succeed at life and still ask, "Is this it?"

We're the only ones who get what we want and realize it's not what we wanted.

That's either a massive evolutionary failure, or we're designed for something beyond the material.

Michael knew the answer. That's why he wanted to trade. He'd filled his life with stuff but his soul was starving. He had everything except the one thing that mattered.

Why Success Makes You More Empty, Not Less

Here's the brutal math of material success:

First million: "I made it!"

Second million: "Now what?"

Third million: "Is this all there is?"

Fourth million: "Why do I feel worse?"

Michael learned what every honest successful person discovers: The more you get, the more you realize it's not enough.

It's like drinking salt water when you're thirsty. Seems like it should work. It's water, right? But the more you drink, the thirstier you get. Eventually, it kills you.

That's success without God. Looks like it should satisfy. It's achievement, right? But the more you achieve, the emptier you feel. Eventually, it destroys you.

Why? Because you're trying to fill an infinite hole with finite stuff.

Imagine trying to fill the Grand Canyon with ping pong balls. You could dump in millions. Billions. Trillions. From ground level, it looks like you're making progress. But from above? You haven't even made a dent.

Your soul is bigger than the Grand Canyon. And you're trying to fill it with ping pong balls:
- Money (ping pong ball)
- Fame (ping pong ball)
- Success (ping pong ball)
- Relationships (bigger ping pong ball, but still)

The Bible says we're made in God's image. That means we have infinite capacity. We're designed for eternal things. We're built for transcendent purpose.

Trying to satisfy that with material success is like trying to survive on cotton candy. It tastes good for a second, then dissolves into nothing, leaving you hungrier than before.

When the Bible Reads You (This Isn't Normal)

I opened Genesis to debunk it. To find contradictions. To prove it wrong.

Instead, it described me perfectly. A 3,000-year-old book knew me better than I knew myself.

That's not normal.

Books don't usually read their readers. But the Bible does this weird thing where:
- You read about pride, and suddenly see yours
- You read about fear, and realize you're terrified
- You read about love, and recognize you don't have it
- You read about sin, and can't deny it's you

It's like the book has X-ray vision for souls.

Here's what's crazy: This happens to everyone.
- Prisoners find themselves in its pages
- CEOs see their emptiness exposed
- Teenagers discover they're not alone

- Skeptics get offended (why, if it's just mythology?)

No other book does this. You can read:
- Plato and get smarter (but not transformed)
- Shakespeare and feel things (but not changed)
- Self-help and get motivated (for about a week)

But the Bible? It does surgery on your soul.

The Bible claims to be "living and active, sharper than any two-edged sword" (Hebrews 4:12). That's either insane or true.

Based on what happened to me (and millions of others), I'm going with true.

When an ancient book accurately diagnoses your exact spiritual condition without knowing anything about you, that's not coincidence. That's supernatural.

The Bible doesn't just contain words about God. It carries the authority of God. That's why it can read you while you're reading it.

You're Not an Accident (The Forming vs. Speaking Thing)

Genesis describes God creating everything by speaking. "Let there be light." Boom. Light.

But with humans? Different story.

"Then the LORD God formed the man of dust from the ground and breathed into his nostrils the breath of life" (Genesis 2:7).

Formed. With His hands. Like an artist with clay.

Breathed. His own breath. His own life.

God spoke stars into existence but got hands-dirty making you.

THAT EXPLAINS SO MUCH:

Why you're weird compared to animals:
- Your dog doesn't paint sunsets
- Your cat doesn't write poetry
- Your goldfish doesn't ponder meaning
- Your hamster doesn't have moral crises

But you? You create things that serve no survival purpose. You make music nobody asked for. You write stories nobody needs. You ask questions that don't help you find food or mates.

Evolution can't explain that. If we're just trying to survive and reproduce, why waste energy on:
- Art that doesn't attract mates
- Philosophy that doesn't find food
- Sacrifice that helps competitors
- Questions about meaning that cause depression

Unless... we're not just trying to survive.

Unless... we're made for more than reproduction.

Unless... we bear the image of a Creator.

That's why you feel special. Not because you're arrogant, but because you ARE special. You're not cosmic accident. You're not random molecules. You're not just smart ape.

You're formed by God, carrying His breath, bearing His image.

No wonder you hunger for more than food.

No wonder you thirst for more than water.

No wonder nothing finite satisfies you.

You're made in the image of the infinite.

Searching for the Voice

WHAT THIS MEANS for You

If you're killing yourself for success:

Stop for a second. Really. Stop.

Ask yourself: If you get everything you're working for, then what?

Promotion? Then what?

Million dollars? Then what?

Perfect relationship? Then what?

Dream house? Then what?

Eventually you run out of "then whats" and you're left with... what?

Michael found out. Don't wait until you've lost your family, your health, and your soul to discover what he discovered: Success without God is failure.

You can gain the whole world and lose your soul. That's not a religious threat. That's a mathematical fact. Infinite loss for finite gain is a terrible trade.

If you feel empty despite having "everything":

You're not depressed. You're not ungrateful. You're not broken.

You're spiritually hungry. And that hunger is a gift.

It's proof you're made for more than this.

It's evidence you have a soul, not just a body.

It's a GPS saying, "Wrong direction. Recalculating."

Don't medicate the hunger. Don't distract from it. Don't fill it with more stuff.

Follow it. It's leading you home.

That restlessness you feel? It's homesickness for a place you've never been but somehow remember. Eden. Heaven. Home. God.

If you think the Bible is just another old book:

Try this experiment:

Read Genesis 1-3. Just three chapters.

But don't read it to judge it. Read it like it might be reading you.

Pay attention to:

- What makes you uncomfortable (why?)
- What rings eerily true (how would ancient writers know that?)
- What describes you perfectly (coincidence?)

If it's just mythology, it should feel like mythology.

If it's just human wisdom, it should feel limited.

If it's just ancient literature, it should feel dated.

But if it feels like it knows you, sees you, and is speaking directly to you...

Maybe it's not just a book.

Maybe it's a message.

Maybe it's God introducing Himself.

What have you got to lose? Three chapters. Twenty minutes. Could change everything.

Or you could stay empty. Your choice.

The teenager reading Genesis alone in his room discovered what Michael's millions couldn't buy: identity, purpose, and relationship with the One who formed us for Himself.

Reflection

What would you be willing to trade for spiritual hunger?

If you already have that hunger, are you feeding it or trying to satisfy it with substitutes?

What does your restlessness tell you about what you were designed for?

The same God who breathed life into Adam is still breathing, still calling, still forming hearts that are willing to be formed by Him.

I'D FOUND God in my closet, but finding Him was just the beginning. Now came the hardest part—learning that the identity I'd been trying to construct was actually something I needed to receive. And that lesson would come through network cables, accidental eavesdropping, and a shoe shiner who knew more about my soul than I did.

[1] C.S. LEWIS, *Mere Christianity* (New York: HarperOne, 2001), 140.

5

BECOMING SOMEONE NEW

The Phone Call That Changed Direction

"Paul, they need you here."

My friend's voice crackled through the phone from Seattle. He'd been at Good Samaritan Practical Missionary School for exactly one week, and already he was recruiting.

"They've got serious network problems. Their whole IT infrastructure is a mess. You're the only person I know who can fix this."

I wasn't interested in Bible school. My brothers had done the missionary training route—that was their path, not mine. I was eighteen, fresh from my Genesis encounter, still sitting in closets talking to God, but formal religious education? That felt like going backward, like trying to systematize something that had just become beautifully personal.

"I'm not enrolling," I said firmly. "But I'll come help with the network."

Famous last words.

The Accidental Student

The drive to Seattle was familiar—I knew Peter Radchuk, who ran the ministry. He was a good man, passionate about training young people for ministry. When I arrived and saw their network setup, I understood why they needed help. Cables everywhere, no organization, outdated equipment, security vulnerabilities that made my eye twitch.

"This will take a few weeks," I told Peter. "Maybe a month."

He smiled. "Take all the time you need. Work during classes if you want—you might find them interesting."

I set up my workspace in the back of the main classroom, running cable, configuring routers, doing what I did best—making systems work. But as I worked, I couldn't help but overhear the lectures.

Monday: "The Nature of God's Love"
Tuesday: "Understanding Biblical Authority"
Wednesday: "Prayer as Relationship, Not Performance"

That last one made me stop crimping cables and listen.

The Youth Pastor's Question

Russell Korets was young for a pastor—maybe late twenties—with an easy laugh and a way of making profound truths sound like common sense. The youth group met in the evenings at the church connected to the school building. I started attending, telling myself it was just convenient since I was already there working.

One Wednesday night, Russell was teaching about relationship with God, and he used an analogy that stopped me cold.

"Imagine we're friends," he said, pacing the small stage.

"Real friends. We hang out, we talk, we know each other's voices. Now imagine we're in Costco—that massive warehouse store where you can barely see from one end to the other. I'm three aisles over and I call your name. What happens?"

A kid in the front raised his hand. "We'd recognize your voice?"

"Exactly! Why?"

"Because we know you."

Russell grinned. "Right. Because we've spent time together. We know each other's voices, patterns, ways of speaking. Now—" he paused, looking directly at me somehow, though I was in the back row, "—how well do you know God's voice?"

The Shoe Shiner's Word

A few days after that youth service, I was walking through downtown Seattle. It was a busy morning—the kind where office workers rush past with coffee cups and tourists crane their necks at the tall buildings. I was crossing at one of those major intersections where the city's energy feels most intense.

On the corner stood one of those old-school shoe shiners, the kind you don't see much anymore. His setup was simple: a wooden box, polish, brushes, and a weathered face that spoke of years watching the city change around him.

As I approached the crosswalk, surrounded by dozens of other pedestrians, this man pointed directly at me.

"You, young man!"

I looked around, confused. In a crowd of people, surely he couldn't mean me.

"Are you talking to me?" I asked.

Searching for the Voice

"Yes," he said with certainty. "I have a word from God for you."

My heart started racing. You have to understand—I was already at that crossroads Russell had been talking about. My heart was softening through the classes I was "accidentally" attending, the youth services, the late-night prayers in my closet back home. The soil of my soul was becoming more tender, more receptive.

I walked over to him, curious and slightly nervous.

"You're wrestling with God," he said, his eyes intense but kind. "You're trying to decide whether to give in or not give in. You're at a crossroads."

I stood there, stunned. This stranger had just described my exact spiritual state with surgical precision. Yes, I had a relationship with God. Yes, I was talking to Him in my closet, building that friendship. But I was also wrestling—holding back parts of myself, trying to maintain control while surrendering others.

"Don't wrestle," the shoe shiner continued. "Just trust Him. He'll lead you to green pastures."

Green pastures. Psalm 23. "He makes me lie down in green pastures. He leads me beside still waters. He restores my soul" (Psalm 23:2-3, ESV).

"Thank you," I managed to say, then turned and walked away, my mind spinning.

Whether this was a prophetic word, a divine appointment, or a remarkable coincidence, I couldn't say with certainty. What I can say is that this man had spoken directly into my exact spiritual situation—words that either revealed supernatural insight or demonstrated an uncanny ability to read a young person's spiritual struggle.

I ducked into a convenience store, bought a few things, and tried to process what had just happened. The whole encounter felt surreal, and I found myself torn between skepticism and wonder.

After about fifteen minutes, I decided to go back. I had questions. I wanted to understand what he meant by "give in," what those green pastures looked like.

But when I returned to the corner, he was gone.

I looked around, checked the adjacent streets, asked other people if they'd seen him. "He left already," someone told me with a shrug.

Standing there on that busy corner, I felt a familiar stirring in my spirit. "Lord, what is this?" I prayed silently. "What do You mean by giving in? What does it mean to trust You completely?"

Whatever the explanation for this encounter—divine orchestration or meaningful coincidence—it felt like another voice calling to me. Just like the stereo speakers I'd searched as a child, here was someone pointing me toward the Voice I'd been searching for all along.

The message was becoming clearer: Stop wrestling. Stop trying to control the outcome. Trust Him to lead you where you need to go.

Green pastures were waiting, but I had to stop fighting for the rocky ground I was trying to maintain control over.

The Hardest Person to **Stop Performing For**

The realization hit me gradually, like dawn breaking: I was still performing.

Yes, I'd had my Genesis moment. Yes, I'd encountered God personally. But somehow, I'd immediately started trying to earn what I'd just been given freely. Reading the Bible became a duty to check off. Prayer became a performance to perfect. Church attendance became a way to prove my commitment.

I was like a child who'd just been adopted, still trying to earn my place at the dinner table.

The apostle Paul (there's that name again) had struggled with the same thing. He wrote to the Galatians: "Are you so foolish? Having begun by the Spirit, are you now being perfected by the flesh?" (Galatians 3:3, ESV).

I'd begun in the Spirit—that night with Genesis, that raw encounter with the God who formed me. But I was trying to perfect it through human effort, through religious performance.

Dietrich Bonhoeffer warned against what he called "cheap grace" in his classic work *The Cost of Discipleship*—treating God's gift as something to be earned after the fact. But there's another error—trying to pay for expensive grace with worthless currency.

THE BOOK About Prayer

In my car, I had an old cassette tape—yes, cassette, like the stereo I'd dismantled years ago. It was an audio version of a book simply called "How to Pray." The author walked through prayer not as a religious obligation but as genuine conversation with a real Person.

Driving between home and the school, I'd listen to that scratchy recording, learning what I should have known all along: God didn't want my performance. He wanted my presence.

"Prayer," the author said through my car's tinny speakers, "is not informing God of things He doesn't know. It's not convincing Him to do things He doesn't want to do. It's aligning your heart with His, learning to want what He wants, to see as He sees."

He Just Wanted My Time

One afternoon, exhausted from running network cables through the ceiling, I sat in the empty classroom. Sunlight streamed through the windows, dust motes dancing in the beams. The silence was profound.

"Lord," I said out loud, "what do you want from me?"

The answer came not as words but as understanding, like warmth spreading through cold limbs:

Time. I just want your time.

Not my achievements. Not my perfect theology. Not my religious performance. Time. Simple, unproductive, "wasteful" time. Like a father who just wants to sit with his child, not accomplish anything, just be together.

Jesus had modeled this. Despite the pressing needs, the crowds, the mission to save the world, He regularly withdrew to spend time with the Father. "And rising very early in the morning, while it was still dark, he departed and went out to a desolate place, and there he prayed" (Mark 1:35, ESV).

If the Son of God needed that time, how much more did I?

The Poem in the Dark

September 7, 2005. 8:25 PM.

The youth service had ended, but I couldn't leave. Russell's words about knowing God's voice had convicted something in me—or perhaps revealed what had been there all along. I pulled out my Bible, found a blank page in the back, and started writing.

The words came like water breaking through a dam, years of performance and pretense crumbling as truth poured out:

A New Life
September 7, 2005 - 8:25 PM
Outside I laugh, inside I cry
Outside I'm strong, inside I'm weak
Outside I'm a Christian, inside I'm far from God
Outside I live, inside I died long ago
My heart is stone, I am lost
No hope, no future—darkness consumes me
One last day, one last coffee
Ready to leave this world behind
Then I saw Him—a man being beaten
I ran to help, but saw myself among those striking Him
"Why?" I cried
"My son," He said, "I die to give you life inside"
Blood on my hands, pain in my body
I woke—this was no dream
New life burns within me now
Thank You, Lord
But my friends—they're still dead inside
Lost and afraid like I once was
Lord, show them Your love
Give them the new life You gave me
Oh friend, don't die inside
He died for you
Let Him bring you back to life

WHEN I FINISHED WRITING, my hand was cramping and tears had smudged some of the ink. This poem—this confession—had poured out of me like blood from a wound that needed to bleed before it could heal.

It was my story in verse: the disconnect between external Christianity and internal death, the desperation of maintaining a facade while dying inside, the encounter with Christ who took my place, the transformation from death to life, and the burden for friends still trapped where I had been.

The performance was over. The real relationship had begun.

Others See What We Cannot

A few weeks after writing that poem, a childhood friend came to visit me in Seattle. We hadn't seen each other for a while, and I was curious what he'd think of this new chapter in my life.

We spent the day together—walking around the city, catching up, talking about old times. But as the afternoon progressed, I noticed him watching me with a strange expression.

Finally, he said something that caught me completely off guard:

"Paul, I'm jealous of who you're becoming. I'm envious of you. I want to have what you have."

I was stunned. "What do you mean?"

"How did you become this person?" he asked. "You're... different. There's something about you that wasn't there before. You seem... settled. Peaceful. Like you found what you were looking for."

I didn't know what to say. I told him I didn't have all the

answers, but that a voice had been calling me to trust, to give in and not wrestle. It was a short conversation, but it stayed with me.

Later, reflecting on his words, I realized something profound: often we don't see ourselves from the outside. When God performs surgery on us, when He begins shaping us into someone new, we're often the last to recognize the transformation. We're too aware of our remaining imperfections, too focused on how far we still have to go.

But others see it. Friends, family, even strangers sometimes notice the change before we do.

Think about it this way: Have you ever looked at old photos of yourself and cringed? Not just at the fashion choices (though those too), but at who you were? That person in the photo is you, but also... not you anymore. Something fundamental has shifted.

That's what my friend was seeing—a shift I was too close to notice. Like trying to watch grass grow, you can't see it happening, but come back a month later and it's obvious.

The changes were subtle at first. Songs I used to love started making me uncomfortable. Not because someone told me they were wrong, but because something inside had changed. It was like developing an allergy to food you once enjoyed—your whole system rejects what it once craved.

Conversations shifted too. Instead of complaining about life, I found myself curious about God's perspective. Instead of gossiping, I wanted to understand people's struggles. Instead of proving I was right, I wanted to learn what was true.

Even my sense of humor changed. Jokes that once seemed hilarious now felt mean. Sarcasm that used to be my second language started tasting bitter. Not overnight—

so gradually I didn't notice until someone pointed it out: "You don't mock people anymore."

The shoe shiner's prophetic word was being fulfilled: I was learning to trust, to stop wrestling, and God was indeed leading me to green pastures. But I needed others to help me see what was too close for me to recognize.

Here's what I learned: Real transformation isn't about trying harder to be different. It's about something deeper changing inside you, like your spiritual DNA being rewritten. You don't have to remember to act like a new person—you just are one.

The old me was becoming too small, like outgrown clothes that no longer fit. Not because I was trying to outgrow them, but because something larger was growing inside me—Christ Himself, expanding my capacity for love, joy, peace, and purpose beyond what I thought possible.

The Living Temple

During one of the classes I "accidentally" listened to while working, the teacher read from 1 Corinthians: "Do you not know that you are God's temple and that God's Spirit dwells in you?" (1 Corinthians 3:16, ESV).

I'd heard this verse a hundred times, but now it connected to Genesis 2—God breathing His breath into humanity. We weren't just meant to visit God's temple; we were meant to BE His temple. His dwelling place. His home.

The teacher continued: "The first Adam walked with God in a garden. The second Adam—Christ—makes it possible for God to walk with us wherever we are. You are the garden now. You are the meeting place."

This wasn't about me achieving something for God. It was about God achieving something in me.

Identity Hidden in Christ

"You have died, and your life is hidden with Christ in God" (Colossians 3:3, ESV).

Hidden. Not displayed, not performed, not earned. Hidden.

Like a child in the womb, completely surrounded, completely dependent, completely safe. My identity wasn't something I had to construct or discover—it was something I received. I was in Christ, and Christ was in me.

This changed everything about how I understood transformation. I wasn't trying to become someone new through self-improvement. I was discovering who I already was in Christ. The work wasn't mine to do; it was mine to receive.

As 2 Corinthians 5:17 declares: "Therefore, if anyone is in Christ, he is a new creation. The old has passed away; behold, the new has come" (ESV).

New creation. Not improved version. Not upgraded model. New.

The Difference Between Self-Help and Transformation

Sitting in that classroom-turned-network-center, I finally understood a crucial theological distinction that had eluded me for years—not that secular methods never produce change (they clearly can), but that the source and ultimate sustainability of transformation reveals deeper spiritual realities.

Self-help approaches, at their best, can generate significant behavioral change through willpower, habit formation, cognitive restructuring, and social support. Psychology has documented genuine success in areas like addiction recovery, anxiety management, and character development. These methods deserve respect and can provide real benefits.

However, there's a fundamental theological difference in both source and sustainability:

Self-help operates from human agency utilizing natural capacities. Even when successful, it requires continuous energy expenditure from finite human resources. This isn't a failure—it's simply the nature of natural transformation working within created limitations.

Spiritual transformation claims supernatural agency working through renewed human nature. The theological assertion is that divine life, once imparted, provides resources beyond natural human capacity. Not that effort disappears, but that the source of transforming power transcends human limitation.

Self-help says, "I can change through applied technique and sustained effort."

Transformation says, "Christ in me can produce change that exceeds my natural capacity."

Self-help focuses on behavior modification through external methods.

Transformation focuses on identity reformation through internal divine presence.

Both can appear successful externally, but the Christian claim is that supernatural transformation provides qualitatively different resources for facing trials, moral challenges, and ultimate questions of meaning that natural methods, however sophisticated, cannot fully address.

Jesus had said it plainly: "Come to me, all who labor and are heavy laden, and I will give you rest. Take my yoke upon you, and learn from me, for I am gentle and lowly in heart, and you will find rest for your souls. For my yoke is easy, and my burden is light" (Matthew 11:28-30, ESV).

The Song That Spoke

Driving home from the school one evening, a song came on the Christian radio station that perfectly captured my journey. The lyrics spoke of imagining what it would be like to finally see God face to face, to move from faith to sight, from hoping to knowing.

As I listened, I realized this was what I'd been searching for all along—not information about God but imagination captured by God. Not facts to master but a Person to know. Not a test to pass but a relationship to receive.

The curiosity that had driven me to dismantle stereos was the same hunger driving me toward God—but now I understood I wasn't searching for components and circuits. I was searching for the Singer Himself.

The Music That No Longer Fit

Another area where I began to notice this "outgrowing" was in my music choices. Before my Genesis encounter, before the closet prayers and the Seattle awakening, I'd been drawn to a particular genre of music that wasn't edifying or spiritually healthy. It was degrading, morally bankrupt—the kind of music that left me feeling dirty after listening to it.

I'd struggled with this for months. I wanted to quit listening to it, but every time I tried, I'd find myself coming back. This was before Spotify or smartphones—we burned CDs back then. I'd create a disc with this music, listen to it in my car, feel guilty and disgusted afterward, then throw the CD away in a moment of conviction.

But a few days later, I'd find myself burning another copy. It became a cycle: create, listen, feel guilty, destroy, repeat.

After my encounter with God, something interesting began to happen. Yes, I'd still make the CD again. But each time I listened, I didn't just feel dirty—I felt like "this isn't me anymore."

Slowly, gradually, like turning down a volume knob notch by notch until the sound becomes mute, my interest in that music began to fade. My taste was changing. What once appealed to me started feeling foreign, like clothes that no longer fit.

This wasn't instant transformation—it was a journey that took nearly a year. The Lord was working naturally, organically, changing my desires from the inside out. Some days I'd still be tempted, but increasingly I'd find myself reaching for worship music instead, or turning off the radio entirely to spend time in prayer.

One day I realized I was no longer addicted to that genre of music at all. The transformation had happened so gradually I almost missed it. But it was complete—those songs that once held power over me now felt like shoes I'd outgrown: too small for who I was becoming.

This idea of outgrowing things became vivid to me years later when I became a father. My oldest son, Gabriel, wanted to grow up so fast. I remember one day when he was about three years old, he came to me frustrated and upset.

"Dad, I'm so small!" he said. "I'm not growing fast enough!"

He wanted to be grown up already, and I didn't know how to comfort him. But then I remembered something—he had a favorite pair of shoes that he loved to wear, but I knew he had grown out of them. They were sitting in his closet, those beloved shoes he used to cherish.

"Gabriel," I said, "why don't you go grab your favorite shoes?"

He ran to his closet, brought them over, and I told him to put them on. He started trying to slip them on—one foot, then the other. He pushed and struggled, trying to force his feet into those shoes, but he couldn't get them on. He became very frustrated.

I paused him for a moment. "Do you know why you can't put them on? Think about it. What's going on here?"

He looked at me, and suddenly his eyes lit up. They got bigger. His frustrated expression transformed into a huge smile, and he became very happy.

"Am I grown?" he asked excitedly. "Does that mean I'm becoming bigger?"

"That's exactly right," I told him. "You are growing up."

From the outside, as his father, I could see what he couldn't see about himself—that he was indeed growing, changing, becoming more than he was before. He needed someone with perspective to point out the obvious transformation happening in his life.

This is exactly what happens in our spiritual lives. We need fellow believers who can observe our growth when we can't see it ourselves. We need the community of faith to say, "Look! You're not the same person you were. Those old behaviors don't fit you anymore because you're becoming someone new."

Just as Gabriel needed his father to help him understand he'd outgrown his shoes, I needed others to help me see that I'd outgrown that destructive music. The songs that once held power over me had become like Gabriel's favorite shoes—too small for who I was becoming in Christ.

My brother Sergey had always told me, "Paul, it's better to grow slowly and naturally in Christ than to be that person who grows artificially quick, because when hardship comes, he deflates and loses direction entirely."

He was right. The journey with Christianity, he'd explained, is better when it's a natural growth process. And my struggle with music was proof of that principle. God didn't flip a switch and instantly change my preferences. He walked with me through the process, letting me experience both the old desires and the new ones, until gradually the new nature won out.

I used to wonder why I didn't have instant transformation testimonies like some people. Why wasn't my deliverance immediate and dramatic? Later in life, I understood: God was developing our friendship through that process. Through the Holy Spirit, He was correcting me, shaping me, teaching me to trust Him with the gradual work of replacing my heart of stone with a heart of flesh.

Every time I chose the better music over the degrading music, every time I threw away that CD and meant it a little more, I was learning what it meant to partner with God in my own transformation. I was discovering that becoming someone new isn't like flipping a switch—it's like learning to walk with Someone who's patient enough to let you stumble while strong enough to keep you from falling.

The process taught me something crucial: when you become a new creation in Christ, even when you fall back into old patterns, you don't remain there. It's not who you are anymore. Your identity has changed, and eventually your behavior catches up to your identity.

As Jesus said about the kingdom of God—it's "already but not yet." It's here now, but still coming in fullness. We see imperfections, we face battles, we experience setbacks.

But in the hearts of those who love Christ, the kingdom is advancing, bringing peace and transformation one volume-knob turn at a time.

CHRIST AS EVERYTHING, Not Number One

My brothers had been right to go on mission trips, to pursue formal ministry training. That was their path. I too would later pursue formal seminary training, but God had first met me in my own way—through network cables and accidental eavesdropping, through poems in the dark and songs in traffic.

The key wasn't the method. The key was the surrender.

"He becomes everything in our life," I'd written in that poem. Not number one on a list where other things are number two and three. Everything. The list itself.

During this time, I had a vivid realization about what it means for Christianity to encompass everything. I started thinking of life like a pizza or pie, with a cross in the center and every slice radiating out from that center.

One slice I'd call education. Another slice, family. Another, entertainment. Career, relationships, hobbies, decisions—each slice of life connected to the center, which was God.

When I understood this, the whole concept of "God is number one" disappeared. It wasn't that Christ was first on my priority list—Christ was the center that gave meaning and direction to every other priority.

My entertainment needed to honor God. My career needed to honor God. My family relationships, my educational choices, my financial decisions—every slice was coherently connected to Him. I could no longer make choices in one area while ignoring God in another. The compartmentalized life was over.

This was what Paul the apostle understood when he wrote, "For to me to live is Christ, and to die is gain" (Philippians 1:21, ESV). Not "to live is to serve Christ" or "to live is to believe in Christ" but "to live IS Christ."

Christ wasn't taking up more space in my life—He was becoming the context for all of it. The integration was total.

I remembered Jim in that Moscow airport, raising his hands to pray in front of strangers. As a young man, I'd put my head down, embarrassed by what seemed weird and shameful. But now I understood what I'd seen in Jim: he didn't care what other people thought because he was completely surrendered. Christ wasn't compartmentalized into a "religious" slice of Jim's life—Christ was the cornerstone of every part of his existence.

That level of integration changes everything about who you are and how you live. When Christ is the center, not just number one, shame disappears because you're not performing for human approval anymore. You're living from a different center entirely.

The Accidental Student Becomes Intentional

I never officially enrolled in that Bible school. But I attended every class while "working on the network." I participated in every discussion while "testing the audio system." I completed every assignment while "making sure the computers could handle the workload."

Peter Radchuk would smile knowingly when he'd see me taking notes in the back. Russell Korets would save me a seat at youth group. My friend who'd called me to help would laugh and say, "I knew you'd end up staying."

They all saw what I was slow to recognize: God had used a network problem to solve my identity problem. He'd used physical cables to teach me about spiritual connections. He'd used a school I didn't want to attend to school me in what I desperately needed to learn.

You don't discover identity. You receive it.

You don't earn relationship. You enter it.

You don't perform for God. You rest in Him.

HIDDEN in Christ Through Every Storm

Later in life, when I became a father and faced the inevitable storms that come with adulthood, I would fully understand what it meant to be "hidden with Christ in God" (Colossians 3:3).

I heard a story once about a young couple on their honeymoon cruise. Partway through their voyage, an announcement came over the ship's loudspeaker: "All passengers must return to their cabins and remain in their beds. We are entering a severe storm."

The couple panicked. They called the information desk, demanding to speak with the captain. Why was the ship heading into the storm instead of away from it? They were filled with anxiety and fear.

When the captain called them back, his response was simple but profound: "I have two things to tell you. First, I'm the captain, so I make the decisions. Second, this ship was designed to go through storms."

That's what it means to be hidden in Christ. Christ was designed to go through storms. When we're hidden in Him, it's no longer us facing the tempest—it's Christ in us, Christ around us, Christ as our vessel and our captain.

Every believer faces storms—some weekly, some daily.

For some, it seems like the storm never ends. But we have to remember that the "cruise liner" we're hidden in—Christ Himself—has already defeated death. He is victorious. He was built to handle every storm we'll ever face.

This isn't self-help. This isn't positive thinking or mental techniques. This is what He can do through us, in us, despite us. When the storms come, and they will, we don't have to panic like passengers who forgot what vessel they're traveling in.

We're hidden in the One who calmed the wind and waves with a word, who walked through His own death and came out victorious on the other side. The same power that raised Christ from the dead is at work in us (Ephesians 1:19-20).

Becoming someone new isn't just about changed behavior or improved character—though those things happen. It's about discovering that your identity is now secured in Someone who cannot be shaken, cannot be defeated, cannot be sunk by any storm.

When Gabriel couldn't fit into his old shoes, it wasn't a tragedy—it was evidence of growth. When I couldn't enjoy my old music, it wasn't a loss—it was proof of transformation. When friends noticed I was becoming someone different, it wasn't because I was trying harder—it was because I was hidden in Someone greater.

I thought I finally understood. But God had one more lesson for that boy who took apart stereos—and this time, the discovery would complete the circle in a way I never saw coming.

APOLOGETICS INSIGHTS & Life Applications

What happened at Bible school wasn't self-improvement. It was something entirely different—and understanding the difference changes everything about how we approach personal change.

WHY NEW YEAR'S Resolutions Fail (But Faith Doesn't)

Let's be honest: How many times have you promised yourself you'd change? "This year I'll stop..." "Starting Monday I'll begin..." "Never again will I..."

And how'd that work out?

You're not alone. Most New Year's resolutions are dead by February. Diets last about three weeks. Gym memberships become donations to the fitness industry. We joke about it, but deep down it hurts—why can't we change?

Here's what nobody tells you: You're trying to push a car that needs to be driven.

Self-help says, "Try harder! Believe in yourself! You've got this!" But you don't got this. If you did, you would have changed already. Every failed attempt proves the same truth: Human willpower is like a phone battery—it always runs out.

But here's where it gets interesting. I've watched drug addicts get completely free. Not managing their addiction, not white-knuckling through each day—free. I've seen marriages everyone wrote off completely restored. I've watched angry people become gentle, anxious people find peace, selfish people discover generosity.

What's the difference? They stopped trying to push the car and let Someone else drive.

When the Bible says, "I can do all things through Christ who strengthens me," it's not a motivational poster. It's explaining the difference between human effort (pushing) and divine power (driving). One exhausts you; the other energizes you. One is temporary; the other is transformational.

The Music Test (How I Know It Was Real)

Here's a weird way to know if change is real or fake: Check what you enjoy.

Anyone can force themselves to stop doing something for a while. But can you make yourself stop wanting it? Can you will yourself to hate chocolate or love brussels sprouts? Try it. I'll wait.

That's why my music transformation was so strange. Nobody gave me a list of "bad songs." Nobody shamed me into change. Over months, songs I used to love started feeling... wrong. Like wearing someone else's clothes. They just didn't fit anymore.

It wasn't just music. Foods I craved lost their appeal. Shows I binged became boring. Jokes I loved seemed mean. Not because I was trying to be holy—I wasn't that disciplined. Something inside had shifted, and my desires followed.

Think about your own life. How many times have you forced yourself to stop something, only to want it even more? That's behavior modification—all pressure, no peace. But when God changes you, the want itself changes. You don't have to remember not to do it; you genuinely don't want to.

I've watched this happen to others:

• My friend who used to live for parties now finds them empty
• A coworker who was addicted to gambling doesn't even think about it
• My neighbor who raged at everything became the calmest person I know

They didn't just change their behavior. Their actual desires transformed. That's not willpower—that's something supernatural happening inside.

The Bible calls it getting "a new heart" (Ezekiel 36:26). Not a repaired heart, not an improved heart—a new one. Like a heart transplant changes what your body accepts and rejects, a spiritual heart transplant changes what your soul craves.

When Others See It First

Want to know if your faith is real? Ask the people who live with you.

It's easy to fake spirituality at church. Smile, say the right things, raise your hands during worship. But at home? At work? In traffic? That's where real change shows up.

My childhood friend saw changes I couldn't see. Not because I was performing for him—I didn't even know he was watching. He noticed because real transformation leaks out in a thousand small ways:

- How you react when cut off in traffic
- What you say when you think no one's listening
- How you treat the server who messed up your order
- What you do with money when no one's counting
- How you handle criticism, failure, disappointment

Here's what's wild: The people around genuinely changed Christians consistently report the same things:

"My husband isn't the same person. He's patient now."

"My mom stopped being so critical. She's actually encouraging."

"My roommate used to be so negative. Now he's the most positive person I know."

"My coworker stopped gossiping. Completely."

These aren't performance reviews. These are confused observations from people trying to explain what they're seeing. They can't understand how someone fundamentally changed without therapy, medication, or self-help programs.

You know what's hard to fake? Consistency. Anyone can be nice for a day. But week after week, month after month, when the "new you" becomes the "normal you," people notice. They might not understand it, they might not like it, but they can't deny it.

That's the difference between trying to be better and being made new. One is exhausting performance; the other is natural overflow. One requires constant effort; the other just happens. One fools some people sometimes; the other transforms your entire life in ways everyone can see.

The Identity Crisis Nobody Talks About

"Just be yourself!"

"Follow your heart!"

"You do you!"

Cool. But what if you don't know who you are? What if your heart keeps changing its mind? What if "you doing you" isn't working?

Here's the exhausting truth about building your own identity: You never finish. Every achievement raises the bar. Every failure threatens the foundation. Every rejection makes you question everything. You're constantly constructing, defending, and reconstructing who you are.

It's like building a house on sand during hurricane season. Good luck with that.

I tried building my identity on:
- Being the smart kid (until I met smarter kids)
- Being rebellious (until rebellion got boring)
- Being successful (until success felt empty)
- Being spiritual (until spirituality became performance)

Each identity worked until it didn't. Each required constant maintenance. Each could be destroyed by one failure, one rejection, one bad day.

Then I discovered something revolutionary: What if identity isn't something you build but something you receive?

The Bible says believers are "hidden with Christ in God" (Colossians 3:3). Hidden. Protected. Secure. Not because of what you've done but because of what He's done. Not based on your performance but on His permanence.

It's like the difference between earning your last name and receiving it at birth. You don't maintain your family membership through achievement. You're in because you're in. Period.

Watch what happens to people who get this:
- They stop needing everyone's approval
- They can fail without falling apart
- They face criticism without crumbling
- They lose achievements without losing themselves

Why? Because their identity isn't in what they do but in whose they are. It's not constructed; it's received. It's not earned; it's given. It's not fragile; it's unshakeable.

What This Means for You

If you keep failing at change:

Here's permission to stop trying so hard. Seriously. Stop.

You're not failing because you're weak. You're failing because you're trying to do God's job. It's like performing surgery on yourself—technically possible but generally a terrible idea.

Instead, try this: Tell God you can't change yourself and ask Him to do it. Then watch what happens. Not overnight—real change is like losing weight, you don't see it daily but suddenly your clothes don't fit.

Pay attention to your desires. When something you used to crave starts losing its appeal, that's God working. When patience shows up where anger used to live, that's transformation. When peace replaces anxiety without you trying, that's supernatural.

If you're exhausted from performing:

What if you could stop auditioning for your own life? What if your worth was already decided, your value already set, your identity already secure?

That's what "hidden in Christ" means. You're not on stage; you're backstage with the Director. You're not proving yourself; you're being yourself—the self God says you are.

Try this for one week: Stop introducing yourself by what you do. Stop measuring your day by what you achieve. Stop apologizing for not being enough. Instead, wake up knowing you're already approved, already loved, already enough.

Watch how exhausting it is at first (performance is a hard habit to break). Then watch how free you become.

If you think this is just psychology:

Fair enough. But answer this: Why do Christians experience consistent personality changes that therapy alone doesn't produce? Why do people with no knowledge of psychology show textbook signs of integrated mental health after conversion? Why does "giving up" produce better results than "trying harder"?

Don't take my word for it. Find someone who's been genuinely transformed by faith—not religious, but changed. Ask their family what's different. Ask their coworkers what shifted. Ask them what it feels like from the inside.

Then ask yourself: What explains this better—psychology or something supernatural?

The young man fixing networks while accidentally becoming a student discovered that true transformation comes not from trying harder but from trusting deeper—in the God who makes all things new.

Reflection

Are you still performing for God, trying to earn what's already been given?

The hardest person to stop performing for isn't your parents, your church, or your community—it's God Himself. But He doesn't want your performance. He wants your presence. He doesn't need your achievements. He desires your time.

What would change if you stopped wrestling and started trusting Him to lead you to green pastures?

What "old shoes" in your life no longer fit the person you're becoming in Christ?

6

A FRUITFUL LIFE AT LAST

The Vine and the Branches
I was twenty-two, three years into my walk with Christ, and so exhausted I fell asleep during my own prayer—again.

Not physically exhausted—spiritually depleted. I'd been running on the hamster wheel of Christian productivity: Bible studies to lead, people to evangelize, programs to support, committees to serve on. My calendar looked impressive. My soul felt empty.

Then one morning, reading through John's Gospel over coffee, I hit chapter 15 like a wall:

"I am the vine; you are the branches. Whoever abides in me and I in him, he it is that bears much fruit, for apart from me you can do nothing" (John 15:5, ESV).

I'd read it before. Quoted it. Even taught it. But this time, the words rearranged something fundamental in my understanding.

Abide. Not achieve. Not accomplish. *Abide.*

I set down my coffee and really looked at the passage. Jesus wasn't talking about productivity. He was talking about connection. The branch doesn't strain to produce grapes—it simply stays connected to the vine, and fruit happens naturally.

I'd been trying to manufacture fruit in my own strength. Squeezing out service, forcing spiritual disciplines, generating good works through sheer willpower. No wonder I was exhausted. I was a branch trying to produce fruit while severed from the vine.

The Bread of Life and Living Water

What I discovered through this season of exhaustion was that Jesus had already given us the solution to spiritual depletion. He called Himself "the bread of life" and promised, "Whoever comes to me shall not hunger" (John 6:35, ESV). He also declared, "If anyone thirsts, let him come to me and drink. Whoever believes in me, as the Scripture has said, 'Out of his heart will flow rivers of living water'" (John 7:37-38, ESV).

These weren't just beautiful metaphors—they were practical realities for daily spiritual life.

Bread sustains. Water refreshes. Both are necessities, not luxuries. You don't eat once and stay full forever. You don't drink once and never thirst again. These are daily needs requiring daily provision.

The same is true with Christ. Abiding in Him isn't a one-time connection—it's a daily discipline, a moment-by-moment dependence. When I'm connected to Him as the source of life, I find the fulfillment my soul craves. Not through achieving more or performing better, but through being surrounded by the One who loves me, cares for me, and loved me first.

This transformed my understanding of spiritual disciplines. Prayer wasn't about finding God's favor—I already had that through Christ. Bible reading wasn't about earning God's approval—I already possessed that as His child. These practices became ways of remaining connected to the Person I was in relationship with, like conversation and shared meals in human friendship.

When you're connected to Christ on this daily basis, something beautiful happens: the living water doesn't just fill you, it flows out of you. The bread doesn't just sustain you, it nourishes others through you. You stop trying to manufacture fruit and start naturally producing it.

The Blanket of Scripture

My pastor friend Samuel had a way of making profound truths simple. We were having lunch one day when I confessed my spiritual exhaustion.

"Paul," he said, setting down his sandwich, "let me ask you something. When you go to bed at night, what do you do when you're cold?"

"Pull up a blanket?"

"Exactly. You don't generate your own heat through effort. You receive warmth from the blanket." He leaned forward. "The Word of God is like that blanket. Every day, pull it over yourself. Study it deeply—use your mind, ask questions, wrestle with difficult passages—but also let it cover you, warm you, transform you. The greatest theologians throughout history combined rigorous scholarship with humble reception."

"Be under the Word, not over it," he continued. "This doesn't mean intellectual passivity—God gave us minds to engage seriously with Scripture. Rather, it means approaching even our most careful study with the recognition that we're students, not judges, of divine revelation. When we try to be over the Word, we're attempting to control its message rather than be shaped by it. But when we're under the Word—combining thoughtful analysis with humble submission—it shapes us, molds us, changes us from the inside out."

That image stuck with me. Every morning, instead of attacking my Bible study like a homework assignment, I began to simply sit under Scripture, letting it wash over me like warmth on a cold night.

NAVIGATING Emotional Seasons

But here's what I learned the hard way: even when you understand these truths intellectually, you'll still go through seasons where emotions try to derail your spiritual stability.

Especially as a young believer, I would get caught in emotional roller coasters, thinking that if I didn't *feel* close to God, He must be upset with me, far away from me, or disappointed in my spiritual performance. Sometimes this was legitimate conviction—I had genuinely crossed boundaries, displeased God by not living out authentic friendship with Him, or betrayed His trust through sin.

But other times, the emotions were simply lying to me.

It's like having a close friend whom you hear rumors and gossip about. Someone tells you, "He said this about you," or "He thinks that about you," and suddenly you're doubting the friendship. But then when you actually talk to your friend face-to-face, he says, "I never said that. I never did that. Those were outside voices trying to break our friendship, trying to put distance between us."

The same thing happens spiritually. Our emotions sometimes listen to different thoughts and voices—condemnation, doubt, accusation—and when we accept these as truth, it hinders our deep relationship with our heavenly Father.

EMOTIONS: **Thermometer, Not Thermostat**

I learned to use a simple principle: emotions shouldn't be the thermostat of our spiritual well-being.

Think about the thermostat in your house or car. You set it to the desired temperature, and it regulates the environment accordingly. Imagine if that thermostat was controlled by your emotions—you'd be adjusting it constantly. One moment you'd feel hot and crank up the air conditioning; the next moment you'd feel cold and blast the heat. Your environment would be chaos.

The same is true spiritually. If we let emotions control our spiritual temperature, we'll be all over the place—hot one day, cold the next, questioning our relationship with God based on how we feel rather than what we know to be true.

Instead, God calls us to use the mind He gave us to honor Him. Let the mind set the thermostat based on biblical truth, and emotions will follow. They won't always follow immediately, and they won't always follow perfectly, but they will come under the control of renewed thinking rather than controlling our spiritual direction.

This doesn't mean emotions are bad—they're beautiful and good, designed by God for us to experience the richness of our Christian walk. Experiencing God emotionally is essential. But emotions should be instruments in the orchestra, not the conductor.

When Emotions Become Gossip Against God

I learned to ask myself: "Are my emotions being used by God to build up this friendship, or are they being used as gossip and slander against the friendship I have with God?"

When emotions magnify God's goodness, celebrate His faithfulness, or deepen my appreciation for His love, they're serving their proper function. When emotions make me doubt God's character, question His promises, or withdraw from His presence based on feelings rather than facts, they're acting like malicious gossips trying to destroy a good relationship.

The key is learning to hold emotions captive to the truth of God's Word rather than letting them take our thoughts captive to their fluctuating messages.

Don't allow emotions to cripple your friendship with God or hinder your abiding in Christ. Instead, let emotions fulfill their proper role: to magnify and enhance the genuine, deep friendship you have with God based on His unchanging character and promises.

Behind the Microphone

The revelation that changed everything came while I was fixing an old recording studio for a friend's church. They wanted to start recording sermons and worship services, so I was setting up the equipment—microphones, mixing boards, the whole system.

As I tested the microphones, speaking into them and hearing my voice come through the speakers in the next room, it hit me: this was exactly what I'd been looking for in that stereo as a child.

The voices in the stereo weren't in the machine—they were in the studio, behind the microphone. The stereo was just the delivery system. The real person, the actual singer, the true source was somewhere else entirely.

All these years, I'd been looking for meaning in the "stereos" of life:
- Career success (a high-quality stereo)
- Financial security (an expensive stereo)
- Relationships (a stereo with good speakers)
- Intellectual achievement (a technically advanced stereo)
- Even religious activity (a "Christian" stereo)

But none of these contained the Voice. They were all just delivery systems, and I'd been taking them apart looking for something that was never there to begin with.

The Author Behind the Microphone

"God doesn't mind you running a successful business," I said to my friend Mike, who was struggling with similar questions. We were at the same coffee shop where I'd written my poem years earlier. "He doesn't mind you being creative, intellectual, successful. Those are all attributes that come from Him."

"But?" Mike asked, knowing there was more.

"But He wants you to know Him—the Person behind the microphone. Not just the echoes of His voice in creation, success, or achievement. Him. The Author Himself."

I thought about all the ways we try to find God in the effects rather than the Source:
- We seek purpose in our work rather than in the One who gives work meaning
- We look for identity in our achievements rather than in the One who achieved everything for us

- We search for fulfillment in relationships rather than in the Relationship we were made for

THE FRUIT WE Cannot Force

The apostle Paul listed the fruit of the Spirit in Galatians: "Love, joy, peace, patience, kindness, goodness, faithfulness, gentleness, self-control" (Galatians 5:22-23, ESV).

Notice he called it "fruit," not "fruits." It's singular. You don't get to pick and choose—"I'll take some joy but skip the patience." It's one fruit with multiple characteristics, and it all comes from one source: abiding in Christ.

I'd been trying to manufacture these qualities:

- Forcing myself to be patient (and failing spectacularly in traffic)
- Attempting to generate joy (which looked more like forced cheerfulness)
- Working hard at being gentle (which came across as artificial softness)

But fruit doesn't come from the branch's effort. It comes from the branch's connection to the vine.

Jesus said it plainly: "Apart from me you can do nothing" (John 15:5, ESV). Not "you can do less." Not "you'll struggle more." Nothing. Zero spiritual fruit apart from abiding in Him.

This was both humbling and liberating. Humbling because it meant all my striving was ultimately futile. Liberating because it meant the pressure was off—I didn't have to manufacture what only God could produce through me.

The Transformation I Couldn't Create

Looking back at my journey—from the curious child dismantling stereos to the young man desperately seeking meaning—I could see the thread God had been weaving all along.

That curiosity? It was meant to lead me to Him.

That hunger for meaning? It was designed to be satisfied in Him.

That emptiness you feel? It was shaped specifically for Him.

But here's what I couldn't see until now: transformation isn't something we achieve. It's something we receive through connection.

When I abide in Christ—really abide, not just visit on Sundays—His life flows through me like sap through a branch. The fruit that appears isn't my fruit; it's His fruit growing on my branches.

Christ-like, Not Christ-Performing

There's a crucial difference between being Christ-like and performing Christianity.

Performance says: "I must act like Jesus."

Transformation says: "Christ in me naturally lives like Jesus."

Performance is exhausting.

Transformation is energizing.

Performance requires constant effort.

Transformation requires consistent connection.

The apostle Paul understood this when he wrote, "I have been crucified with Christ. It is no longer I who live, but Christ who lives in me" (Galatians 2:20, ESV).

Notice he didn't say, "I try really hard to live like Christ."

He said Christ literally lives in him. The Christian life isn't imitation; it's inhabitation.

The First Year of the Branch

My gardener friend explained something about grapevines that revolutionized my understanding of spiritual growth.

"The first year," he said, showing me his young vines, "these branches won't produce any fruit. They're just receiving life, establishing their connection, growing strong. If they tried to produce fruit too early, it would damage them."

"So what do they do the first year?" I asked.

"They abide. They receive. They grow. The fruit comes later, naturally, when they're ready."

This freed me from the pressure I'd put on myself and others. New believers aren't supposed to immediately produce abundant fruit. They're supposed to connect, receive, grow. The fruit comes naturally as the connection deepens.

Hidden in Christ

"Your life is hidden with Christ in God" (Colossians 3:3, ESV).

Hidden. Not displayed, not performed, not advertised. Hidden.

This concept transformed my understanding of identity, but it requires careful biblical balance to avoid extremes—we don't lose our humanity or personality, yet we're genuinely transformed by God's presence within us.

The doctrine of union with Christ represents one of

Christianity's most powerful truths. When we accept Jesus as Lord and Savior, something miraculous happens—we become one with Him spiritually. It's like a branch grafted into a vine, maintaining its identity while drawing life from a new source. We remain fully ourselves while Christ lives in and through us.

Think of it this way: when the Holy Spirit fills us, we're not replaced or absorbed—we're empowered, transformed, renewed. Paul said it clearly: "I have been crucified with Christ. It is no longer I who live, but Christ who lives in me" (Galatians 2:20, ESV). Yet in the same breath, he adds, "And the life I now live in the flesh I live by faith in the Son of God." We're still us, but we're new creations inhabited by God's Spirit.

This spiritual union happens through faith and is sustained by the Holy Spirit's power. We become "partakers of the divine nature" (2 Peter 1:4, ESV) not through religious performance or special knowledge, but through simple faith in Jesus and the transforming work of the Holy Spirit. It's available to everyone who believes—no exceptions, no prerequisites except faith.

The Bible describes it as being "in Christ"—a phrase that appears over 150 times in the New Testament, showing this isn't just theology but lived reality. Through faith, we are:

- Loved in Christ (Ephesians 1:4) - chosen because God loves every person
- Redeemed in Christ (Ephesians 1:7) - salvation freely offered to whosoever believes
- Made alive in Christ (Ephesians 2:5) - spiritual life available to all through faith
- Created for good works in Christ (Ephesians 2:10) - empowered by the Spirit for purpose

- Brought near in Christ (Ephesians 2:13) - intimate relationship through grace

This union actually increases our freedom and authenticity. When you know you're loved unconditionally, accepted completely, and empowered supernaturally, you're free to be who God created you to be. The Holy Spirit doesn't make us robots—He empowers us to live abundantly. Because our identity is secure in Christ's finished work, we can take risks, love boldly, and serve freely without fear of losing God's love. This security produces the confidence and joy that marks Spirit-filled living.

ALPHA AND OMEGA

"I am the Alpha and the Omega," says the Lord God, "who is and who was and who is to come, the Almighty" (Revelation 1:8, ESV).

Alpha and Omega—the first and last letters of the Greek alphabet. In English, we'd say "A to Z." Christ is the beginning and the end, and here's the beautiful part: we're all the letters in between, hidden in Him.

My story, your story, every human story—we're all contained within His greater story. We don't write our own narratives; we discover our place in His.

BORN TWICE

Pastor Adrian Rogers once said something that stuck with me: "In a world where everyone is born once, Christians are unique—we're born twice."[1]

Jesus explained it to Nicodemus: "Unless one is born again he cannot see the kingdom of God" (John 3:3, ESV).

The first birth is physical—we enter the world.

The second birth is spiritual—we enter the kingdom.
The first birth gives us biological life.
The second birth gives us eternal life.
The first birth makes us human.
The second birth makes us children of God.

This second birth isn't just a religious experience or a moral transformation. It's a fundamental change in our nature, our identity, our very being. We become "new creations" (2 Corinthians 5:17), not improved versions of our old selves.

What I Would Tell That Boy

If I could sit down with that six-year-old boy carefully removing screws from a stereo, searching desperately for the voices inside, here's what I'd say:

"Paul, you're looking in the right direction but the wrong place. Those voices you're searching for? They're not in the machine. They're in the studio, behind the microphone.

"All your life, you'll be tempted to search for meaning in the machines—in success, in relationships, in achievements, in knowledge. You'll take apart every stereo life offers, looking for the Voice that makes it all make sense.

"But here's the secret: The Voice you're looking for isn't hidden in the machine. He's calling to you through it. Every question you ask, every system you dismantle, every answer you seek—they're all leading you to the Person behind the microphone.

"When you finally meet Him—and you will—you'll discover that the meaning you've been searching for isn't something you achieve or discover or create. It's Someone you know. And in knowing Him, you'll finally understand who you are.

"You're not just a curious boy who takes things apart. You're a beloved son, created to know your Father, designed to bear His fruit, destined to display His glory.

"Keep searching, but know that the One you're searching for is already searching for you. And He's closer than the voices in the stereo."

THE ONGOING JOURNEY

Christianity isn't a moment; it's a journey. It's not a one-time decision; it's a daily abiding. It's not about reaching a destination; it's about deepening a relationship.

Every day, I still have to choose:

- Will I try to produce fruit, or will I abide in the Vine?
- Will I perform Christianity, or will I be inhabited by Christ?
- Will I search for meaning in the machines, or will I know the Person behind the microphone?
- Will I let my emotions be the thermostat, or will I let God's truth set the temperature?

The struggle isn't over. The performance tendency still whispers The temptation to find identity in achievement still calls. Emotions still try to convince me that God's love fluctuates with my spiritual temperature.

But now I know the secret: Life has meaning not when we achieve something but when we abide in Someone. True fruit comes not from trying harder but from staying connected. Real transformation happens not through self-improvement but through Christ-inhabitation. And genuine spiritual stability comes not from emotional consistency but from anchoring our souls in unchanging truth.

The living water still flows. The bread of life still sustains. The Vine still produces fruit through willing branches. Not because of our performance, but because of His presence. Not because we feel it every moment, but because we can trust it every moment.

This is what it means to live a fruitful life at last—not a perfect life, not a life without emotional ups and downs, but a life rooted in the unshakeable reality that we are loved, chosen, sustained, and empowered by the One who is Himself the meaning we've been searching for all along.

Stay Hungry for the Meaning of Life

I end every blog post, every podcast, every conversation about faith with the same phrase: "Stay hungry for the meaning of life."

But now you know what I really mean: Stay hungry for Christ, because He IS the meaning of life.

Not Christianity as a religion.

Not church as an institution.

Not theology as an academic pursuit.

Christ Himself. The Person. The Voice behind the microphone. The Vine to which we're connected. The Alpha and Omega in whom we're hidden.

Jesus said, "I am the way, and the truth, and the life" (John 14:6, ESV). Not "I'll show you the way" or "I'll teach you the truth" or "I'll give you life." I AM these things.

He is what we've been looking for all along.

The boy taking apart the stereo was searching for Him.

The teenager exploring different beliefs was seeking Him.

The young man offended by the Gospel was being drawn to Him.

And now, the man writing these words has found in Him

what no amount of searching, achieving, or performing could provide:

Meaning. Purpose. Identity. Life.

Not because I figured it out, but because He revealed Himself.

Not because I achieved it, but because He achieved it for me.

Not because I found Him, but because He found me.

And He wants to find you too.

I thought my search was over. But God had saved the most important lesson for last—a message not just for me, but for every seeker who would come after. If you've made it this far, you need to hear what comes next.

Apologetics Insights & Life Applications

I was exhausted from trying to be a good Christian. Three years in, and I was running on fumes. That's when I discovered the difference between performing faith and living it—and why only one of them lasts.

The Secret of Not Burning Out

Ever feel like the Christian life is exhausting? Like you're constantly failing at being good enough? Like faith is more tiring than your job?

You're not alone. And you're not weak. You're just doing it wrong.

I know because I did it wrong for years. My spiritual life looked like this:

- Wake up feeling guilty for not praying enough
- Try harder to read the Bible

- Fail at being patient by 9 AM
- Promise to do better tomorrow
- Repeat until exhausted

Sound familiar?

Here's what nobody told me: I was trying to be the vine instead of the branch.

Think about a grapevine for a second. You ever see a branch sweating, straining, grunting to squeeze out grapes? "Come on, just one more grape!" Of course not. That would be insane. Branches don't produce fruit through effort. They produce fruit by staying connected.

But that's exactly what I was doing spiritually—trying to squeeze out love, joy, peace through sheer willpower. No wonder I was exhausted. I was trying to generate what I was meant to receive.

The Bible says it plainly: "I am the vine; you are the branches. Whoever abides in me and I in him, he it is that bears much fruit, for apart from me you can do nothing" (John 15:5). Not "you can do less." Not "it's harder." Nothing.

That's either the most depressing news ever (you can't do anything) or the most liberating (you don't have to). I've decided it's liberating.

Why Other Religions Burn Out But Faith Doesn't

Every religion has devoted followers who eventually hit a wall. The Buddhist monk who meditates for decades but still struggles with desire. The Muslim who prays five times daily but finds no peace. The Hindu yogi seeking enlightenment but never arriving. The self-help junkie always one book away from breakthrough.

Why do they all burn out while genuine Christians can go strong for 50+ years?

It's not about trying harder. It's about the source of power.

Think of it like this: Other religions are like training for a marathon—you can get better, go longer, push harder, but eventually you hit your limit. Your muscles fail. Your willpower cracks. You collapse.

Christianity is like being plugged into a power source. You're not generating the energy; you're receiving it. You're not the battery; you're the device being powered.

Every other system says: "Try harder, dig deeper, reach higher."

Christianity says: "Plug in and receive."

Every other system depends on your strength, which always runs out.

Christianity depends on God's strength, which never does.

I've watched this play out:

- Former meditation practitioners who say Christianity brought the peace meditation promised
- Ex-Muslims who found in Christ the intimacy with God they'd always sought
- Former atheists who discovered that rationalism couldn't sustain meaning through suffering
- Reformed addicts who tried every program but only found freedom through faith

The difference? They stopped trying to generate spiritual life and started receiving it. They stopped being the power source and became the conduit. They stopped performing and started abiding.

WHEN YOUR FEELINGS Lie to You (And Why That's Normal)

Here's something Instagram won't tell you: Your feelings are terrible GPS.

"Follow your heart!" they say. Cool. My heart has told me:

- God must hate me (after a bad day)
- I'm a spiritual failure (when tired)
- Everyone else is doing better (thanks, social media)
- God has abandoned me (during depression)
- I should give up (approximately weekly)

If I followed my heart, I'd have quit faith 100 times by now.

But here's what changed everything: realizing emotions are thermometers, not thermostats.

A thermometer tells you the temperature. It doesn't control it.

A thermostat sets the temperature. It determines reality.

Your emotions are great thermometers—they tell you what's going on inside. Feeling distant from God? Good information. Feeling overwhelmed? Worth noting. Feeling doubtful? Important data.

But emotions make terrible thermostats. They shouldn't set your spiritual temperature. They shouldn't determine truth. They shouldn't control your faith.

God's truth is the thermostat. His Word sets reality:

- He loves you (even when you don't feel it)
- You're forgiven (even when shame screams otherwise)
- He's with you (even when you feel alone)
- You're His child (even when you feel rejected)

This isn't "positive thinking." This is choosing truth over feelings. And surprisingly, when you consistently set your thermostat to truth, your emotional thermometer eventually follows. Not immediately. Not perfectly. But gradually, your feelings align with reality instead of fighting it.

The Bread and Water That Actually Satisfy

Jesus made a weird claim: "I am the bread of life" and "Whoever drinks the water I give will never thirst again."

Either He was crazy, or He knew something about sustainable satisfaction that we're missing.

Think about every other satisfaction source:
- Success? Great until the next goal
- Money? Never quite enough
- Relationships? People disappoint
- Experiences? The high always fades
- Achievement? Someone's always doing better

They're all like junk food—tastes great, satisfies briefly, leaves you hungrier.

But here's what I discovered: When Jesus called Himself "bread" and "water," He wasn't being poetic. He was explaining sustainability.

Bread and water aren't luxuries. They're necessities. You need them daily. You never outgrow needing them. And when they're good quality, they genuinely satisfy.

That's what abiding in Christ is like. It's not a spiritual sugar high that crashes. It's not a motivational energy drink that stops working. It's daily bread—sustainable, necessary, satisfying.

This isn't religious talk. This is lived experience. The "bread of life" actually fills you. The "living water" actually quenches thirst. Not metaphorically. Really.

And unlike every other satisfaction source, this one doesn't run out, doesn't get old, doesn't disappoint. Because it's not based on what you do but on who He is.

What This Means for You

If you're exhausted from trying to be "good enough":

Stop. Just stop.

You're trying to squeeze water from a rock. You're trying to be your own life source. You're trying to be God.

No wonder you're tired.

Try this instead: Tomorrow morning, instead of promising God you'll do better, tell Him you can't. Instead of striving to produce fruit, ask Him to produce it through you. Instead of performing for Him, just be with Him.

It feels wrong at first—like you're being lazy. But watch what happens when you stop striving and start abiding. The fruit you couldn't force starts growing naturally. The peace you couldn't manufacture just shows up. The joy you couldn't generate begins flowing.

Not because you're trying harder, but because you finally stopped trying to be the source.

If your faith feels like it's always running on empty:

You might be running on the wrong fuel.

Self-powered spirituality always runs out. Always. It's like trying to run your phone without ever charging it—you can manage your battery perfectly, close all your apps, dim your screen, but eventually it dies.

Plug in. That's what abiding means. Stay connected to the power source. Make it daily, make it regular, make it normal. Not complicated spiritual gymnastics—just connection.

Read Scripture like you're hungry, not like it's homework. Pray like you're talking to someone who likes you, not interviewing for a job. Worship like you're grateful, not auditioning.

The difference between exhausting religion and sustainable faith? One runs on your power; the other runs on His.

If you think all religions are basically the same:

Test this: Find a devoted practitioner of any religion and ask them, "Does it get easier or harder over time?"

Most will say harder. More disciplines, more requirements, more effort.

Now ask a mature Christian the same question. They'll likely say something strange: "It gets easier because I stopped trying so hard."

That's the difference. Every other system requires more from you over time. Christianity requires less of you and more of Christ. Every other system depends on your strength increasing. Christianity depends on your dependence increasing.

Don't believe me? Look at elderly believers. While other religions often see declining participation with age (can't maintain the disciplines), Christianity often sees increased joy and peace. Why? Because it never depended on their strength in the first place.

The exhausted young man trying to manufacture Christian fruit learned what I believe speaks to a broader human condition: the struggle between self-sufficiency and dependence on something greater. Our role is not to produce life but to receive it, not to generate fruit but to bear it, not to create meaning but to abide in the One who IS meaning.

REFLECTION

What "stereos" are you still dismantling, searching for the Voice inside?

What if the meaning you're seeking isn't hidden in the machine but is calling to you through it?

What if the fruit you're straining to produce would grow naturally if you simply stayed connected to the Vine?

And what if the emotional roller coaster you're on isn't an indicator of God's love for you but simply the voice of gossip trying to destroy a friendship based on unchanging truth?

The invitation isn't to try harder but to abide deeper. Not to perform better but to be inhabited more fully. Not to let emotions be your spiritual thermostat but to let God's truth set the temperature of your soul. Will you stop trying to be the vine and accept your place as a branch?

> "Abide in me, and I in you. As the branch cannot bear fruit by itself, unless it abides in the vine, neither can you, unless you abide in me." — Jesus Christ (John 15:4, ESV)

---

[1] ADRIAN ROGERS, "Born Twice, Die Once" (sermon, Bellevue Baptist Church, Memphis, TN).

7
WHAT I WOULD TELL MY YOUNGER SELF

Three Versions of Paul

If I could gather them in one room—miraculous as that would be—I'd bring together three versions of myself.

The six-year-old with a screwdriver in hand, surrounded by stereo parts.

The sixteen-year-old with questions that wouldn't stop, wrestling with worldviews.

The twenty-year-old in a closet, finally talking to God like He was really there.

And here's what I, the forty-something Paul who's walked this road longer, would tell them. Not lectures. Not sermons. Just truth wrapped in love, wisdom born from wandering, and hope grounded in experience.

To the Boy with the Screwdriver

Little Paul, I see you there on the living room floor, so careful with each screw, so methodical with each piece.

You're not breaking things—you're searching for something. And that search? It's holy.

Adults will misunderstand. Some will praise your curiosity, others will punish it. You'll get mixed messages about whether questions are good or dangerous. Let me tell you now: your questions are gifts. Every single one.

That stereo you're taking apart? You won't find the singers inside. I know that disappoints you. But here's the secret: you're not really looking for singers. You're looking for the Singer. The One whose voice echoes in every melody, whose creativity sparked yours, whose curiosity planted yours.

Those circuits and wires that fascinate you? They're sermons in copper and silicon, each connection preaching about the Connection you were made for. You see, God doesn't mind that you take things apart. He designed you to. He gave you that beautiful, restless mind because He wants to be found, and He delights in children who seek.

But Paul, remember this: Some things can't be understood by dismantling them. Love doesn't make sense when you dissect it. Grace can't be diagrammed. And God—the One you're really searching for—He reveals Himself not to those who take Him apart but to those who let Him put them together.

Keep that screwdriver. Keep that curiosity. But know that the greatest discoveries won't come from what you deconstruct but from Who reconstructs you.

To the Teenager with All the Questions

Sixteen-year-old Paul, I know how heavy those questions feel. Why does Leo believe differently? Why can't Ivan accept your gift? Why do all these religions claim to have the truth? Why doesn't Christianity look like the Book of Acts anymore?

You're standing at the crossroads of a thousand worldviews, and each one has billboards advertising satisfaction. Buddhism promises enlightenment. Islam offers submission and peace. Atheism claims intellectual freedom. Even Christianity, as you've known it, feels more like tradition than transformation.

Here's what I wish I could have told you then: You're not wrong to explore. God isn't threatened by your investigation. In fact, He's the One driving it. Every question you ask is a knock on heaven's door, and despite what you fear, He's not annoyed by the knocking—He's delighted by it.

"You will seek me and find me, when you seek me with all your heart" (Jeremiah 29:13, ESV). Did you catch that? It's not "if" you seek with all your heart, it's "when." God expects the all-in search. He designed you for it.

But let me save you some time and heartache by sharing what I discovered through careful study: While many religious traditions contain sophisticated theology and genuine insights about the divine—Buddhism's profound understanding of suffering, Islam's emphasis on divine mercy and submission, Hinduism's complex metaphysics of the transcendent—there remains a fundamental distinction that sets Christianity apart.

Yes, Buddhism speaks of compassion from bodhisattvas, but these are enlightened beings who achieved their status through accumulated merit. Islam teaches of Allah's mercy, but access depends on human submission and righteous deeds weighing favorably at judgment. Hinduism offers paths of devotion (bhakti), but ultimate liberation requires the soul's realization of its divine nature through spiritual effort across multiple lifetimes.

These are not simplistic "human attempts"—they're sophisticated theological systems developed by brilliant minds across centuries. But here's what Bill Shaker was trying to tell you: Christianity alone presents God taking the initiative to bridge the gap through the Incarnation. Not human beings climbing toward the divine, but the divine descending to become human. Not earning favor through accumulated merit, but receiving unmerited grace. Not realizing our inherent divinity, but having divine life freely given to finite creatures who remain creatures.

The theological term is *gratia sola*—grace alone. While other traditions may speak of divine compassion or mercy, Christianity uniquely teaches that salvation is entirely God's work, achieved through Christ's substitutionary atonement and applied through faith alone (*sola fide*). This isn't cultural arrogance—it's doctrinal precision. The cross represents something qualitatively different: not God showing us the way to reach Him, but God reaching down to us at infinite cost to Himself.

And those friends of yours—Ivan, Leo, your atheist buddy? Love them. Not as projects to convert but as people to cherish. Your job isn't to win arguments but to live such a transformed life that they ask you about the hope within you (1 Peter 3:15).

One more thing: That hunger you feel? That emptiness inside? It's not a flaw. It's a feature. You were designed with a God-shaped hole so that when He fills it, you'll know it's Him and not something else.

To the Young Man in the Closet

Twenty-year-old Paul, sitting there in the dark among your hanging clothes, finally real with God—this is where everything changes. Not in the spectacular moments but in the secret ones. Not in the public proclamations but in the private prayers.

You're about to learn something that will take years to fully grasp: Christianity isn't about getting God to do what you want. It's about God getting you to become who He created you to be.

That performance pressure you feel? That exhausting effort to be "good enough" for God? You can let it go. I know that sounds impossible. I know every religious bone in your body says you have to earn this. But that's exactly what makes the Gospel good news—it's not about your performance but His.

You're going to mess up. Spectacularly sometimes. You'll have seasons where you feel distant from God, where prayers feel like they're bouncing off the ceiling, where you question if that Genesis encounter was even real. Here's what I need you to know: God's grip on you is stronger than your grip on Him.

"My sheep hear my voice, and I know them, and they follow me. I give them eternal life, and they will never perish, and no one will snatch them out of my hand" (John 10:27-28, ESV). That includes you not being able to snatch yourself out.

Stop trying to manufacture fruit. Stop trying to generate spiritual experiences. Stop trying to be the vine when you were designed to be a branch. Your job is simple: Abide. Stay connected. Receive what flows from Him.

And that network job at the Bible school? Take it. Not for the education but for the transformation. God's about to teach you that sometimes He uses ethernet cables to illustrate eternal connections.

The Truth About Your Journey

Here's what all three versions of me need to know: Your story isn't random. That curiosity, that hunger, that relentless search for meaning—it's all been orchestrated by the One you're searching for.

You think you're looking for God, but the truth is He's been pursuing you all along. Every question was His invitation. Every doubt was His opportunity to prove Himself faithful. Every wrong turn was His chance to demonstrate that He's the God who leaves the ninety-nine to find the one.

The stereo you dismantled? He was teaching you that external things can't contain internal realities.

The religions you explored? He was showing you that human effort can't reach divine standards.

The conviction you felt? He was preparing you to receive grace you couldn't earn.

The Genesis encounter? He was revealing that you were known before you knew, loved before you loved, pursued before you pursued Him.

The Lies You Believed

Let me expose the lies that haunted each version of you:

The Lie to the Child: "Your questions make you difficult."

The Truth: Your questions make you human. God gave them to you.

The Lie to the Teenager: "You have to figure this out on your own."

The Truth: The Holy Spirit is your teacher, guide, and revealer of truth.

The Lie to the Young Man: "You have to perform to be accepted."

The Truth: You're accepted in the Beloved, performance not required.

The Lie You Still Fight: "Your worth is in what you accomplish."

The Truth: Your worth was settled at the Cross.

The Community That Sees Your Growth

Years later, as a father watching my son Gabriel struggle with his own growth, I learned something profound about spiritual development that I wish I could have told all three versions of myself.

Gabriel was about three years old when he came to me, frustrated and upset. "Dad, I'm so small! I'm not growing fast enough!" He wanted to be grown up already, to be big like the older kids.

I didn't know how to comfort him at first. Then I remembered his favorite shoes sitting in his closet—shoes he'd outgrown but still loved. "Gabriel, why don't you go grab your favorite shoes?" I suggested.

He ran to get them and tried to put them on, struggling and getting more frustrated as they clearly didn't fit. Finally, I asked gently, "Do you know why you can't put them on? Think about it. What's going on here?"

I watched understanding dawn on his face. His eyes got bigger, his frustrated expression transformed into a smile. "Am I grown?" he asked excitedly. "Does that mean I'm becoming bigger?"

"That's exactly right," I told him. "You are growing up."

As his father, I could see from the outside what he couldn't see about himself—that he was indeed growing, changing, becoming more than he was. He needed someone with perspective to point out the obvious transformation happening in his life.

This is exactly why we need community in our spiritual lives. We need fellow believers who can observe our growth when we can't see it ourselves. Jesus said, "If we walk in the light as he is in the light, we have fellowship with one another" (1 John 1:7, ESV). The concept is simple but profound: we need the constant presence of fellow believers who can uphold each other, help each other grow, and remind us when we're being transformed.

Too often, we're like Gabriel with his shoes—frustrated that we're not growing fast enough, unaware that we've actually outgrown our old patterns, old sins, old ways of thinking. We need the community of faith to say, "Look! You're not the same person you were. Those old behaviors don't fit you anymore because you're becoming someone new."

In our individualistic culture, we often think spiritual growth is a private matter. But Scripture paints a different picture—we grow best in community, where others can see what we can't, encourage what we doubt, and celebrate what we take for granted.

Natural Growth vs. Quick Solutions

If I could give one piece of advice to young readers facing similar struggles to what I experienced, it would be this: understand that faith is not a switch you flip on and off. It's a process of development where God works throughout your life to create you into a new person.

Remember, Christians are people who are born twice in a world where everyone else is born once. Just as a child in the womb goes through nine months of growth and development before birth, spiritually we go through time where we grow and mature into the people God created us to be.

Don't get upset when you struggle and fail. Don't throw in the towel thinking, "This doesn't work. I can't do this on my own." Of course you can't do it on your own—you need Christ! But here's what I've learned: Christ sometimes allows you to try your own strength just so you can see that you can't, and then you come back to Him saying, "Lord, let's work on this together."

My advice? Allow natural growth. Don't buy into the trap of quick solutions. Quick solutions don't exist—they're illusions that redirect you from the longer, more sustainable goal. You see this everywhere: in athletics, in bodybuilding, in academia, in every area of human development. Time is what makes the process coherent and lasting.

I've watched too many people seek the spiritual equivalent of crash diets or get-rich-quick schemes. They want instant transformation, immediate spiritual maturity, rapid deliverance from all their struggles. But just as my brother Sergey told me years ago, "It's better to grow slowly and naturally in Christ than to be that person who grows artificially quick, because when hardship comes, they deflate and lose direction entirely."

Allow God to work with you, through you, and educate you into maturity. Be consistent in Him. Be present with Him. Be available for Him. Find daily time—and here's a practical tip I give young people: every time you eat, get in the habit of reading. Pull up your phone, open a Bible app, or read the Word of God. Study it thoughtfully, ask questions, engage your mind, but also let it transform your heart. Grow daily, daily, daily. Be under that warm blanket of Scripture that gives you warmth through both intellectual understanding and spiritual nourishment, keeps you growing in knowledge and character, and helps you stay in God's presence.

What Never Changes

Through all these years, from that boy with the stereo to the man writing these words, some things remain constant:

The Questions Continue: You'll never stop wondering, exploring, seeking to understand. That's not a lack of faith —that's the shape faith takes in a curious mind.

The Hunger Remains: Even filled, you'll hunger for more of God. C.S. Lewis called it "the inconsolable longing."[1] It's the ache for Eden, the homesickness for heaven, the groaning for glory.

The God Who Answers: He's the same yesterday, today, and forever (Hebrews 13:8). The God who breathed into Adam still breathes life into dead things. The God who walked in Eden still walks with those who seek Him. The Christ who died and rose still lives and intercedes.

To You, Dear Reader

But this chapter isn't really for my younger selves. They've already walked their roads, asked their questions, found their answers. This chapter is for you.

Maybe you're the child, taking apart life's stereos, looking for meaning in the mechanics.

Maybe you're the teenager, overwhelmed by options, confused by competing truths, wondering if there's really a God who cares about your questions.

Maybe you're the young adult, exhausted from performing, tired of pretending, ready for something real.

Or maybe you're none of these and all of these—just a

human being with that same spiritual emptiness, that same inconsolable longing, that same hunger for meaning that drives every human heart.

How This Journey Shaped My Family Life

The journey I've shared with you didn't end when I found God—that's where it truly began. Every experience, every lesson learned through dismantling stereos and wrestling with worldviews and learning to abide rather than achieve, has shaped me in ways I'm still discovering.

It formed me as a father. Watching my children ask their own questions, I remember what it felt like to be dismissed or misunderstood for curiosity. So when Gabriel takes apart his toys or my daughter asks why the sky is blue for the hundredth time, I see echoes of that six-year-old boy with the screwdriver. I've learned to nurture their questions rather than silence them, to see their curiosity as holy ground rather than inconvenience.

It shaped me as a husband. Those years of learning what real love looks like—not performance-based acceptance but unconditional commitment—taught me how to love my wife more deeply. I'm still learning to be the husband and father I want to be. I still see shortcomings that need improvement. I constantly remind myself that I need to be the man who reflects Christ, who allows Christ to be seen through me.

But here's what I want you to understand: this is still a journey. It's not a destination you reach and then coast. Every day I wake up and choose again to be the branch rather than try to be the vine, to abide rather than achieve, to receive rather than perform.

And you know what? The same God who met a six-year-old boy searching in stereo speakers, who pursued a teenager through his questions, who encountered a young man in a closet—He's still working in my life today. The journey of transformation never ends; it just gets richer, deeper, more beautiful.

FOR THOSE WHO Feel Captive

I need to address something specifically for those of you reading this who feel stuck, captive to habits or sins that seem to hold you prisoner. Maybe you're thinking, "Paul's story is nice, but you don't know my struggles. You don't understand how far I've fallen or how many times I've failed."

Here's what I want you to remember: Jesus said He came to set the captives free. He came for those who are sick, to make them well. If you desire freedom, if you can say, "Lord, I need You," He will rescue you. He will give you hope.

This isn't about achieving perfection or having your life together. This is about allowing the One who is perfect to work in your imperfection. This is about letting the One who has His life together put your scattered pieces back together.

Yes, you can become a godly father one day. Yes, you can become a godly wife. Or maybe you already are one but feel like you're failing. You can bear the image of Christ because you are made in the image of God. He loves you. He longs to transform you, to make you whole and new again.

The journey I've shared—from searching to finding to growing—it's available to you too. Not because you're good enough, but because He is. Not because you've earned it, but because He's given it freely. Not because you can do it on your own, but because He promises to never leave you or forsake you.

Don't let the enemy whisper that you're too far gone, too broken, too addicted, too lost. Remember, this whole story started with a God who pursues the lost, who finds the searching, who transforms the broken. That's who He is. That's what He does.

And He wants to do it for you.

Keep Asking, But Know Who Answers

Here's my final word to you, the same words I speak to every version of myself: Keep asking. But know Who answers.

Don't stop questioning—that's how you grow.

Don't stop seeking—that's how you find.

Don't stop knocking—that's how doors open.

But understand this: The Answer isn't a philosophy. It's a Person.

The Answer isn't found in taking things apart but in being put together by the One who formed you.

The Answer isn't hidden in the machine but stands behind the microphone, calling your name.

This wasn't about multiple paths to the same destination. Jesus had already declared the exclusivity that offends and saves there is only one way to the Father, and He is that way.

The Invitation

So here's my invitation—not from me but through me, from the One who's been pursuing you through every page of this story:

Come as you are—curious, skeptical, broken, searching.

Come with your questions—He's not afraid of them.

Come with your doubts—He's bigger than them.

Come with your performance exhaustion—He offers rest.

Come with your spiritual emptiness—He's the only One who fits.

The Gospel isn't complicated: God loves you. You've separated yourself from Him through sin. He bridged the gap through Christ. You can cross that bridge through faith.

"For God so loved the world, that he gave his only Son, that whoever believes in him should not perish but have eternal life" (John 3:16, ESV).

Whoever. That includes you. Wherever you are in your journey, whatever stereos you're dismantling, whatever questions you're asking—you're included in "whoever."

The Continuing Story

My story doesn't end with finding God. That's where it begins. Every day, I'm still that boy with the screwdriver, that teenager with questions, that young man learning to abide instead of achieve.

The difference is now I know: Life's meaning was never hidden in the machine. It was calling to me through it—a Person, not a principle.

And He wants to be known by you.

So take apart your stereos. Ask your hardest questions. Explore every worldview. But remember—you're not searching for components and circuits. You're searching for the Singer behind the song, the Author behind the story, the God who is Himself the meaning you seek.

He's closer than you think. He's been pursuing you through every question, every moment of wonder, every restless night.

Even through this book.

The question isn't whether He's real or whether He cares or whether He has a plan for you.

The only question is: Will you let Him find you?

Your younger self is waiting for your answer.

More importantly, so is He.

And remember—you don't have to have it all figured out. You don't have to grow up spiritually overnight. You don't have to become perfect before you come to Him. You just have to be willing to let Him work in you, through you, and with you for as long as it takes.

Because He's patient with the process. He delights in gradual growth. He celebrates every small step forward, every moment of connection, every choice to trust Him a little more.

The same God who took time to form you in your mother's womb will take time to form Christ in you. The same God who spent years preparing you for this moment will spend years growing you into the person He created you to be.

Trust the process. Embrace the journey. And know that the One who began a good work in you will be faithful to complete it.

A Final Prayer

Lord, for every reader who's made it this far—the curious, the skeptical, the hungry—I pray: Draw them to Yourself. Don't let them go. Whatever it takes, bring them to You.

For those taking apart stereos: Show them they're looking for You.

For those comparing worldviews: Reveal Yourself as the Way.

For those exhausted from performing: Give them rest in Your finished work.

For those ready to surrender: Give them courage to step into the closet and finally, honestly, talk to You like You're really there.

Because You are.

You always have been.

In Jesus' name, the Name above all names, the Answer to all questions, the Meaning behind all meaning.

Amen.

But wait—there's something I haven't told you yet. Something about my friends Ivan, Leo, and the atheist. Something about where they are now and what their journeys taught me about the exclusive truth of Christ, and how the community of faith played a role in all our stories. You need to hear how their stories ended...

Apologetics Insights & Life Applications

My journey from childhood curiosity through teenage questioning to adult faith reveals profound truths about human development and God's design for how we come to know Him. The "three versions of Paul" framework provides compelling evidence for Christianity's unique understanding of spiritual development across the human lifespan.

The Developmental Apologetic: Comparative Analysis of Spiritual Seeking

If I could gather three versions of myself in one room—the 6-year-old with the screwdriver, the 16-year-old with questions, and the 26-year-old finding answers—I'd see something amazing: God meets us exactly where we are, at every age.

Faith for Every Age (Why God Speaks Kid, Teen, and Adult)

Here's something nobody tells you: Your spiritual journey isn't random. It follows a pattern. And that pattern is a clue.

Think about it:

- **Kids** ask ultimate questions ("Who made God?")
- **Teens** test different answers ("What if Buddhism is right?")
- **Young adults** hit crisis points ("Is this all there is?")
- **Mature adults** share what they've learned ("Let me tell you what I discovered")

This happens everywhere. Every culture. Every generation.

That's weird. Unless it's designed.

Other religions try to explain this:

- **Buddhism:** "You're discovering suffering leads to enlightenment"
- **Islam:** "You're naturally drawn to submit to Allah"
- **Hinduism:** "Your soul is recognizing its divine nature"
- **Atheism:** "Evolution made you curious for survival"

But only Christianity explains why:

- Kids specifically wonder about a PERSON ("Who made this?")

- Teens specifically rebel against RELATIONSHIP ("Why should I obey?")
- Adults specifically hunger for PERSONAL meaning ("Does anyone care?")
- Elders specifically share PERSONAL testimony ("Let me tell you about Him")

It's always personal. Always relational. Always about Someone, not something.

That's because we're made for relationship with a personal God, not:
- Enlightenment (impersonal state)
- Submission (one-way obedience)
- Absorption (loss of self)
- Evolution (no meaning at all)

My journey from taking apart stereos to finding God wasn't unique. It's the journey we're all on. The only question is whether we'll recognize Who's been calling us at every stage.

Gabriel's Shoes (How Others See Your Growth First)

My son Gabriel taught me something profound when he was three. He came to me frustrated: "Dad, I'm not growing!"

I had him try on his favorite old shoes. They didn't fit anymore.

"Why won't they fit?" I asked.

His face lit up: "Because I'm BIGGER!"

That's exactly how spiritual growth works. You can't see it happening, but suddenly your old life doesn't fit.

And here's the key: Others see it first.

You're staring at yourself daily, like watching grass grow. Nothing seems different. But people who see you weekly or monthly? They notice:

Searching for the Voice

- "You seem more peaceful"
- "You don't complain like you used to"
- "Something's different about you"
- "You're easier to be around"

This isn't just feel-good nonsense. It's evidence.

If Christianity was just psychological self-help, only YOU would notice changes (placebo effect). But when multiple people independently observe transformation they can't explain? That's external validation of internal reality.

I've watched this happen:

- Angry people becoming gentle (coworkers shocked)
- Selfish people becoming generous (family confused)
- Anxious people finding peace (friends asking "What happened?")
- Bitter people forgiving (enemies bewildered)

They didn't announce "I'm changing!" Others announced it for them: "You've changed."

That's the difference between trying to change (exhausting performance) and being changed (natural transformation). One you have to maintain. The other just happens, like Gabriel growing out of his shoes.

Why Instant Transformation Is Usually Fake

Everyone wants the spiritual microwave. Zap! Transformed!

- "Attend this weekend seminar!"
- "Say this prayer 7 times!"
- "Feel the energy shift!"
- "Manifest your best self!"

Then Monday comes. Nothing's different. So you try the next thing.

Here's the truth: Real growth is like real growth. Slow.

Think about it:
- Babies don't become adults overnight
- Seeds don't become trees in a day
- Muscles don't develop from one workout
- Wisdom doesn't come from one experience

Why would spiritual growth be different?

The Bible uses biological language on purpose:
- "Born again" (starting as spiritual infant)
- "Grow in grace" (gradual process)
- "Bearing fruit" (seasonal, not instant)
- "Being transformed" (ongoing, not once)

Fake transformation is exhausting because you have to maintain the act.

Real transformation is restful because you're actually changing.

Fake requires constant effort to appear different.

Real happens naturally as you become different.

The Weird Thing About Christian Growth (Everything Gets Better)

When I became a Christian, something strange happened. Everything improved:
- Better husband (without marriage seminars)
- Better father (without parenting books)
- Better worker (without career coaching)
- Better friend (without social training)

That's weird. Unless...

Unless there's one thing wrong with us that affects everything. And fixing that one thing fixes everything else.

The Bible calls it sin. Not just bad behavior. The broken connection with God that breaks everything else.

When that gets fixed, everything connected to it improves
- You love better (connected to Love Himself)
- You parent better (understanding Father God)
- You work better (working for eternal purpose)
- You relate better (seeing others as God's image)

It's like fixing the foundation of a house. You don't have to fix every room individually. Fix the foundation, and all the rooms stabilize.

That's why genuine Christians often excel in multiple areas simultaneously. Not because they're trying harder in each area. Because they fixed the one thing that affects all areas.

A Letter to Each Version of You

To the Curious Child (Age 6-12):

Those big questions you ask? Keep asking.

"Why is there something instead of nothing?"

"What happens when we die?"

"Who made God?"

Adults might get frustrated. They might give quick answers to make you stop. Don't stop.

Your questions are clues. You're asking because you're designed to find answers. Not easy answers. Real answers. And the Answer is a Person who loves curious kids like you.

One day, you'll discover that every question was leading you to Him.

To the Searching Teen (Age 13-19):

I know you're testing everything. Good. Test it all.

Test Buddhism (does desirelessness actually work?).

Test atheism (does meaninglessness satisfy?).

Test hedonism (does pleasure fulfill?).

Test Christianity (does it actually transform?).

But test honestly. Don't just test to rebel. Test to find truth.

And when you're done testing, notice which one:
- Explains your actual experience
- Offers real hope (not just cope)
- Changes people (not just their behavior)
- Loves you before you change

Your rebellion might actually be your search for God in disguise.

To the Crisis-Point Adult (Age 20-40):

You got everything you wanted. Now what?

The job, the relationship, the achievement. Still empty.

That's not failure. That's success. You successfully discovered what doesn't work. Now you're ready for what does.

Stop trying to fill the Grand Canyon with ping pong balls. Stop drinking salt water for thirst. Stop building your identity on sand.

The crisis isn't the problem. It's the invitation. God often meets us when we've exhausted all other options.

To the Wisdom Years (40+):

You've learned so much. Share it.

Tell the 6-year-old their questions matter.

Tell the teenager their search is sacred.

Tell the young adult their crisis is an opportunity.

But most importantly, tell them all: The journey is worth it. The seeking leads somewhere. The questions have an Answer.

And He's been pursuing them all along, at every age, in every stage, through every question and crisis and discovery.

Because that's what love does. It pursues at every age until it's found.

The boy with the screwdriver, teenager with questions, and young man in the closet demonstrate that the God who created us with innate curiosity is the same God who satisfies that curiosity with Himself—providing the most adequate explanation for universal human experience across all life stages.

---

[1] C.S. LEWIS, *The Weight of Glory* (New York: HarperOne, 2001), 30-31.

EPILOGUE

The Only Way, The Only Truth, The Only Life
"And this is eternal life, that they know you, the only true God, and Jesus Christ whom you have sent" (John 17:3, ESV).

These words of Jesus have become the foundation of everything. Not a philosophy. Not a religious system. Not one path among many. THE way to know THE only true God through THE only Savior.

I understand this exclusivity offends modern sensibilities shaped by religious pluralism. The objection is predictable: "How can you claim one religion is exclusively true? Isn't that arrogant? What about sincere believers in other faiths?" These are serious philosophical challenges that deserve serious answers.

First, the logical foundation: Truth by its very nature is exclusive. If Buddhism claims there is no permanent self (anatta) and Christianity teaches eternal souls, both cannot be simultaneously true. If Islam denies Christ's divinity and Christianity affirms it, logical consistency demands one is correct and the other mistaken. Religious pluralism—the idea that all religions are equally valid paths to the same destination—violates basic logic by requiring contradictory truth claims to coexist.

Second, the epistemological foundation: The claim "no religion can have exclusive truth" is itself an exclusive truth claim that refutes all religions making such claims. Religious relativism is self-defeating—it absolutizes the relative by claiming absolutely that no absolutes exist in religious matters.

Third, the historical foundation: Christianity's exclusivity isn't based on cultural superiority or religious preference, but on historical claims about specific events—particularly Christ's incarnation, death, and bodily resurrection. These are either historically factual or they're not. If Jesus rose from the dead, Christianity's claims about His unique identity as God incarnate are validated. If He didn't, Christianity is false regardless of its moral teachings or cultural benefits.

Let me be crystal clear about something that might have seemed ambiguous in my journey: When I explored Buddhism, Islam, atheism, and other worldviews, I wasn't shopping for truth in a spiritual supermarket where all options were equally valid. I was investigating competing truth claims through careful study and personal experience. Every path I explored—while containing partial insights and sincere practitioners—ultimately led to philosophical dead ends or unfulfilled promises. Only in Christ did I find answers that satisfied both intellectual scrutiny and existential hunger.

The Friends I Left Behind

You've met Ivan, my Jehovah's Witness friend who couldn't accept my Christmas gift. Leo, the Buddhist who feared stepping on his grandmother's reincarnated soul. My atheist buddy who argued so passionately against a God he claimed didn't exist.

What happened to them?

Ivan continues his sincere pursuit of what he believes to be truth, knocking on doors with genuine zeal for God. His dedication to Scripture study and evangelistic passion demonstrate the authentic spiritual hunger that drives human seeking. Yet the very zeal that compels him reveals Christianity's central apologetic principle: sincerity, while admirable, cannot validate error. Paul the apostle recognized this when he wrote about those who have "zeal for God, but not according to knowledge" (Romans 10:2, ESV). Ivan's earnest seeking actually validates my thesis—the human heart was designed to search for the Voice, but without proper revelation, even sincere seeking can be misdirected. His devotion to a different gospel (Galatians 1:6-7, ESV) demonstrates that the hunger is universal and authentic, but satisfaction requires the true Source.

Leo's continuing spiritual journey—from Buddhism to New Age syncretism—provides perhaps the most powerful apologetic evidence for the universal spiritual emptiness in every human heart. Here is someone who never stopped seeking, never ceased his pursuit of enlightenment and meaning. His very restlessness proves the point: the human heart seeks infinitely, but finite systems cannot satisfy infinite longing. Buddhism's sophisticated philosophy couldn't fill the void, so he added more elements, still searching. This persistent spiritual hunger across traditions demonstrates that we're not dealing with cultural conditioning but universal design. Leo embodies the truth that "the Light shines in the darkness" (John 1:5, ESV)—his seeking itself testifies to the reality of what he seeks, even as spiritual blindness prevents recognition (2 Corinthians 4:4, ESV).

Rashid's faithful devotion to five daily prayers represents sincere submission to what he understands of the divine. His regularity, discipline, and heart for the God of Abraham demonstrate authentic spiritual hunger and genuine reverence for the transcendent. From an apologetic perspective, Rashid's devotion validates several crucial points: first, that the human heart naturally seeks divine relationship; second, that this seeking expresses itself in worship and submission; third, that partial revelation can inspire genuine devotion while remaining incomplete. His sincere worship of Allah as he understands Him actually supports Christianity's claim about universal revelation—"He has not left himself without witness" (Acts 14:17, ESV). Every prayer he offers validates the reality of the God he seeks to serve, the same God who "in these last days has spoken to us by his Son" (Hebrews 1:2, ESV).

My atheist friend provides the most compelling apologetic case of all. Years after I moved away, I received an unexpected message: he'd become a Christian—a genuine, Bible-believing follower of Christ. "Paul," he told me, "you placed small rocks in my walking shoes. All those talks we had at work, all those debates—they led me to look deeper into Christianity."

His conversion validates several crucial apologetic principles. First, that passionate denial often masks deeper seeking—his vehement arguments against God actually demonstrated engagement with ultimate questions that pure materialism cannot answer. Second, that intellectual honesty eventually encounters Christianity's explanatory superiority—as an engineer, he recognized that theism provides better foundations for logic, mathematics, and scientific inquiry than materialistic naturalism. Third, that the persistent "voice" calling through conscience, beauty, and rational investigation eventually demands response. His brilliant engineering mind, trained in evidence evaluation and logical analysis, concluded that Christianity offered the most coherent worldview.

What seemed like fruitless arguments were actually apologetic seeds taking root in intellectually honest soil. The same rational faculties that made him successful in engineering ultimately led him to recognize design pointing to a Designer, moral obligations pointing to a Lawgiver, and existential longings pointing to their fulfillment in Christ. He discovered that gaining the whole world of professional success meant nothing without gaining his soul through grace (Mark 8:36).

Where This Journey Led

As I write these words nearly two decades after that Genesis encounter in my childhood bedroom, I marvel at God's faithfulness. The boy who dismantled stereos became a man who helps build God's kingdom. The teenager who questioned everything became an adult who stands firm on biblical truth. The young man learning to abide became a father teaching his children the same lessons.

God used every piece of my journey—even the wandering, even the doubt, even the performance-driven years. Nothing was wasted. Every question prepared me to give answers. Every wrong turn taught me to appreciate the right path. Every season of spiritual exhaustion equipped me to help others find rest in Christ.

The network cables I ran at that Bible school led to a career in technology, but more importantly, they taught me about spiritual connections that last forever. The discipline learned from that ex-Marine general in Siberia shaped how I parent my children and lead in ministry. Even the music transformation—that gradual change from degrading songs to worship—prepared me to help others navigate their own areas of needed growth.

Marriage taught me about covenant love in ways that deepened my understanding of Christ's love for His church. Parenting showed me the Father's heart in ways no theological study could. Career challenges taught me to live out faith in the workplace. Each season built on the previous one, all orchestrated by the God who wastes nothing in the lives of those who love Him.

The Community That Carried Me

One thing I couldn't have anticipated in those early years was how crucial Christian community would become. Remember Gabriel's shoes—how he needed his father to point out growth he couldn't see in himself? The same principle has played out repeatedly in my spiritual life.

There was Jim in that Moscow airport, whose bold prayer life challenged my timid faith and showed me what complete surrender looked like. There was Russell, the youth pastor whose question about knowing God's voice pierced through my performance and led to authentic relationship. There was Bill Shaker, patiently mentoring a questioning teenager with recommended reading and wise conversation.

But community wasn't just about learning from others— it became about serving others too. Teaching Sunday school forced me to articulate my faith in ways that deepened my own understanding. Leading Bible studies meant I had to live out what I was teaching. Mentoring young men showed me how far God had brought me and how much I still needed to grow.

The shoe shiner's words about trusting God to lead me to green pastures resonated deeply with my subsequent experience. But those green pastures weren't solitary—they were shared with brothers and sisters in Christ who walked alongside me, challenged me, encouraged me, and helped me see God's work in my life when I was too close to recognize it myself.

If you respond to the Gospel message in this book, don't try to live the Christian life in isolation. God designed us for community. Find a Bible-believing church. Connect with other believers. Let them see your growth when you can't, and learn to recognize God's work in their lives too.

Living the Daily Reality

The concepts I've shared in this book—abiding instead of achieving, being a branch rather than trying to be the vine, letting emotions be a thermometer rather than a thermostat—these aren't just philosophical ideas. They're daily realities that require constant choosing.

Every morning, I still have to decide: Will I try to manufacture spiritual fruit, or will I stay connected to the Vine and let Him produce fruit through me? Will I let my emotions dictate my spiritual temperature, or will I let God's truth set the thermostat of my soul?

The daily habits I mentioned—reading Scripture during meals, prayer as relationship rather than performance, seeing every aspect of life as a slice of the pizza with Christ at the center—these practices have sustained me through career changes, parenting challenges, ministry difficulties, and personal struggles.

Here's what I've learned about spiritual growth: it really is more like Gabriel outgrowing his shoes than flipping a light switch. Some changes happen so gradually you don't notice them until someone else points them out. Other transformations feel dramatic in the moment but prove to be just one step in a longer journey.

The key is consistency, not perfection. Daily connection with God through His Word and prayer. Regular fellowship with other believers. Honest confession when you fall short. Grateful acknowledgment of God's grace in your life. These simple practices, maintained over years, produce the kind of deep spiritual maturity that can weather any storm.

The Exclusive Claims I Can't Compromise

Through my journey, I discovered why Christianity offends: it's exclusive. Radically, offensively, beautifully exclusive.

Jesus didn't say, "I am A way"—He said, "I am THE way, THE truth, and THE life. No one comes to the Father except through me" (John 14:6, ESV, emphasis added).

Peter, filled with the Holy Spirit, declared, "And there is salvation in no one else, for there is no other name under heaven given among men by which we must be saved" (Acts 4:12, ESV).

Paul wrote, "For there is one God, and there is one mediator between God and men, the man Christ Jesus" (1 Timothy 2:5, ESV).

This isn't arrogance. This isn't narrow-mindedness. This is truth. And truth, by definition, excludes falsehood.

About Those Prayers You Pretended Not to Hear

If you grew up with praying parents, you know what I'm talking about. The bedtime prayers you rolled your eyes at. The grace before meals that seemed endless. The "I'm praying for you" that felt more like pressure than love.

I think often of my father, slipping into our rooms at 4 AM, praying over his children by name. For years, I was annoyed by it. Now I realize those prayers were seeds that took decades to grow.

If your parents are still praying for you—even if their faith feels foreign to you right now—those prayers matter. They're not manipulation. They're love in its purest form. "The prayer of a righteous person has great power as it is working" (James 5:16, ESV).

You might be running from God right now, but your parents' prayers are following you. And maybe, just maybe, that's actually a gift.

The Businessman's Deal Revisited

Remember Michael, the successful businessman who wanted to trade his companies for my spiritual hunger? I met him again five years after my conversion. The emptiness in his eyes had been replaced with something I recognized: life.

"I couldn't manufacture the hunger," he told me over coffee. "But God created it. I just had to stop filling it with everything else."

He'd lost one company in the process of finding Christ. His ex-wife still wouldn't speak to him. His kids were slowly warming up to the father who'd finally stopped worshipping success.

"Was it worth it?" I asked.

He smiled. "I gained Christ. What else matters?"

Paul the apostle understood: "Indeed, I count everything as loss because of the surpassing worth of knowing Christ Jesus my Lord" (Philippians 3:8, ESV).

The Ongoing Journey

Some might think finding Christ is the end of the story. It's actually the beginning. Every day, I'm still that curious boy, but now I know where to direct my questions. Every day, I'm still taking things apart, but now I'm letting God put me back together.

The difference? I'm not searching for meaning—I'm living from meaning. I'm not trying to fill the spiritual emptiness—I'm letting God fill it fresh each day. I'm not performing for acceptance—I'm resting in being accepted.

The Father's Legacy

Remember my father, slipping into our rooms at 4 AM to pray over his children? Now I understand what he was doing. He was modeling what it means to be a spiritual father—not just providing for physical needs but interceding for eternal ones.

Today, I find myself doing the same thing. Early mornings before work, I'll stand by my children's beds and pray:

"Lord, I pray for Gabriel. Help him grow strong in faith. Guide his steps. Use his questions to lead him to You."

"I pray for Naomi. Protect her heart. Let her know how precious she is to You. May she always walk in Your light."

"I pray for each of my children, that they would know You personally, not just know about You from family tradition."

The faith I discovered through dismantling stereos and wrestling with worldviews is now being passed to the next generation—but not as pressure or performance expectation. As invitation and example.

When Gabriel takes apart his toys with the same methodical curiosity I once showed, I don't discourage it. I see it as holy ground, as the same God-given drive that led me to seek and find. When my children ask hard questions about faith, I remember how Bill Shaker never gave me easy answers but pointed me to better questions.

The goal isn't to protect them from doubt but to show them where doubt can lead when honestly pursued. It's not to give them a faith without questions but to demonstrate that the God we serve isn't threatened by questions—He's the answer questions lead to when followed with integrity.

This is how faith truly reproduces: not through religious performance but through authentic relationship. Not through inherited tradition but through personal encounter with the living God. Not through family pressure but through the natural fruit of a life truly transformed by grace.

But let me be honest: following Christ hasn't answered all my questions. If anything, it's raised new ones. Why does God allow suffering? Why doesn't He save everyone? Why is the path so narrow?

Some questions won't be answered this side of eternity. But I know the One who holds the answers, and that's enough. As Corrie ten Boom said, "Never be afraid to trust an unknown future to a known God."[1]

A Necessary Clarification

My journey of questioning was not deconstruction—it was construction. I wasn't tearing down Christian faith; I was building it on solid ground. Every doubt I wrestled with led me deeper into orthodox Christianity, not away from it. This book stands firmly on historic biblical truth, not trendy spirituality that discards inconvenient doctrines.

Neither is this story about self-empowerment or human potential. I found meaning not by discovering my best self, but by dying to self and finding life in Christ. The transformation described here came through divine grace, not self-improvement techniques.

The Clear Gospel

Let me leave no room for misunderstanding. The meaning of life isn't found in being a good person, following religious rules, or exploring spiritual options. It's found in this truth:

We are sinners — "All have sinned and fall short of the glory of God" (Romans 3:23, ESV). This includes me, you, everyone. Our best efforts are contaminated by sin.

The penalty is death — "The wages of sin is death" (Romans 6:23a, ESV). Not just physical death, but spiritual separation from God for eternity.

Christ paid the price — "But God shows his love for us in that while we were still sinners, Christ died for us" (Romans 5:8, ESV). Jesus, the perfect Son of God, took our punishment.

Salvation is by grace through faith — "For by grace you have been saved through faith. And this is not your own doing; it is the gift of God, not a result of works, so that no one may boast" (Ephesians 2:8-9, ESV).

You must respond — "If you confess with your mouth that Jesus is Lord and believe in your heart that God raised him from the dead, you will be saved" (Romans 10:9, ESV).

This isn't one option among many. This is THE option. Jesus is not a way to God—He is THE way to God. There is no Plan B.

Your Genesis Moment Awaits

Remember my night with Genesis 1-3, when familiar words became God's personal message to me? That same God wants to speak to you. Not through mystical experiences or emotional manipulation, but through His Word and by His Spirit.

Maybe you're exploring faith for the first time, comparing worldviews. Investigate thoroughly—examine the evidence, test the claims, ask the hard questions. But also remain open to the possibility that God might reveal Himself as both the object of your investigation and the Person who has been seeking you all along.

Maybe you grew up in church but faith feels like performance, not relationship. Jesus said, "Come to me, all who labor and are heavy laden, and I will give you rest" (Matthew 11:28, ESV). Your questions and struggles aren't obstacles to faith—they can become doorways to deeper understanding.

Maybe you're full of questions and doubts. Excellent. Keep asking—honest questions honor the God of truth. Pursue your doubts with the same rigor you'd apply to any important inquiry. But as you investigate, remain open to discoveries that might surprise you. The strongest faith often emerges from the deepest questioning, and God is big enough to handle your toughest concerns.

Maybe you've been running from the faith of your childhood. The God you're running from might not be the real God at all.

THE FINAL CHALLENGE

The stereo is dismantled. The search has led to its conclusion. The Voice behind the microphone has been identified. The question now is the same one Pilate faced, the same one every human must answer:

"What will you do with Jesus?"

Will you continue searching in empty stereos, or will you acknowledge the Singer?

Will you keep trying to manufacture meaning, or will you receive it from the One who IS meaning?

Will you remain dead in religion, or will you come alive in relationship?

John 17:3 defines eternal life as knowing the only true God through Jesus Christ. Not knowing about Him. Not agreeing with facts about Him. Knowing Him—personally, intimately, eternally.

This knowledge isn't something you achieve. It's something you receive. It doesn't come from taking things apart but from letting God put you together. It's not found in the machine but in meeting the Person behind the microphone.

He's calling your name. He's been calling all along—through your questions, through your emptiness, through your searching, even through this book.

The meaning of life is not a what. It's a Who.

His name is Jesus.

And He is the only way.

A Final Word

To my children, who will one day read these words: Your father was once a boy who took apart stereos, searching for voices that weren't there. By God's grace, I found the Voice that matters. My prayer—prayed over your beds in early mornings just as my father prayed over mine—is that you would know Him too. Not because it's our family tradition, but because He is truth. Not because I believe, but because He is worthy of belief.

I pray that when you face your own seasons of questioning—and you will—you'll remember that questions aren't the enemy of faith. They're often faith's beginning and can become faith's strengthening. When you encounter different worldviews in school or work, I pray you'll investigate with the same thoroughness I once did, asking hard questions, examining competing claims, and testing everything—confident that truth not only can withstand scrutiny but actually grows stronger through honest examination. Don't fear doubt; fear intellectual dishonesty. Don't avoid tough questions; avoid superficial answers.

And when you inevitably struggle with your own performance-based living, your own attempts to earn what's been freely given, I pray you'll remember the lessons I learned about abiding rather than achieving, about being branches rather than trying to be the vine.

To everyone still searching: Stay hungry for the meaning of life. But know that Jesus Christ IS that meaning. Not part of it. Not one aspect of it. He IS the way, the truth, and the life.

If this book has stirred something in your heart, don't let it settle. If questions have been raised, pursue them honestly. If the Gospel has offended you, consider that the offense might be God's kindness leading you to repentance.

If you've recognized your own story in these pages—the curiosity, the searching, the spiritual emptiness—know that the same God who pursued me is pursuing you.

The stereo is dismantled. The search has revealed its answer. The Voice has been identified. Now the question is yours to answer: What will you do with Jesus?

There is no other.

There has never been another.

There will never be another.

"Jesus Christ is the same yesterday and today and forever" (Hebrews 13:8, ESV).

In Him alone is found the meaning of life—abundant, eternal, and free.

Come and drink.

The invitation stands. The door remains open. The Voice still calls.

And those of us who have found the answer continue to pray that you'll find Him too—not as an abstract concept or philosophical system, but as the Person He is: the Christ who saves, the Lord who transforms, the Friend who never leaves.

The meaning of life isn't a what.

It's a Who.

And His name is Jesus.

Apologetics Insights & Life Applications

After decades of searching, I've reached the most offensive conclusion possible: Jesus is the ONLY way to God. Not a way. THE way. That offends almost everyone today, but math doesn't care about your feelings.

Why "All Roads Lead to God" Is Actually Cruel

Let me tell you what happened to my friends who took different roads:

Ivan (Jehovah's Witness): Forty years of knocking on doors, studying Watchtower magazines, following every rule. Still searching. Still unsure. Still working to earn what he can't achieve.

Leo (Buddhism/New Age Mix): Meditation retreats, crystal healing, chakra alignment, past-life regression. Each new technique promises "This is it!" None deliver. He keeps adding more systems because none work.

My Atheist Friend: Spent years proving God doesn't exist. Won every debate. Lost all meaning. Eventually found Christ because atheism answered no ultimate questions—just eliminated them.

Notice the pattern? Only one road led home.

Here's the brutal truth: Saying "all roads lead to God" sounds kind, but it's actually cruel. It's like telling someone lost in the desert, "Any direction works!" when only one path leads to water.

When your friends are dying of thirst, you don't give them false hope. You give them the real directions.

Christianity says Jesus is God.

Searching for the Voice

Islam says Jesus is not God.
They can't both be right.
2+2=4. Not 5. Not "whatever feels true to you." 4.

Same with ultimate truth. Either Jesus is who He claimed to be or He isn't. Either He's the way or He's not. Either He rose from the dead or He didn't.

Math doesn't become false because people disagree with it.

Truth doesn't become relative because it hurts feelings.

The Math Problem With "Your Truth"

"That's your truth, but I have my truth."

Sounds nice. Doesn't work.

Here's why: "All truth is relative" is an absolute statement. You're absolutely sure that nothing is absolutely sure. That's self-defeating logic.

If everything is relative, then:

- You can't condemn Hitler (just his truth)
- You can't celebrate love (just your preference)
- You can't say murder is wrong (just your opinion)
- Words lose all meaning

But you DO condemn evil. You DO celebrate love. You DO believe some things are actually wrong. Which proves you know some truths aren't relative.

Truth excludes falsehood. That's what makes it truth.

If I say "There's a red car in my driveway" and you say "There's no car in your driveway," we can't both be right. We can check. One of us is wrong.

Jesus said, "I am THE way, THE truth, THE life. No one comes to the Father except through me" (John 14:6).

That's either:

1 True (He is the only way)

2 False (He's lying or deluded)

It can't be "true for some people but not others."

Either there's a car in the driveway or there isn't.

Either Jesus is the only way to God or He isn't.

Either He rose from the dead or He didn't.

The evidence points to TRUE. Historical documents, eyewitness accounts, transformed lives, prophecies fulfilled, empty tomb, disciples willing to die for what they saw.

But even if you disagree with the evidence, you can't disagree with the logic: If Jesus' claims are true, all other claims about salvation are false. That's not mean. That's math.

The Test Every Human Fails (Except One)

Remember Michael? Millionaire who wanted to trade everything for my spiritual hunger?

He tried the "all roads lead to success" approach:
- Made millions (still empty)
- Built an empire (still meaningless)
- Achieved the dream (still a nightmare)

Every road failed. Only Christ worked.

Here's the universal test: Try to satisfy yourself with anything other than God.

Go ahead. Try it:
- Money? Ask any rich person who's honest
- Fame? Check celebrity rehab centers
- Power? Look at politicians' faces
- Relationships? Ask any divorced person
- Experiences? Talk to any world traveler
- Knowledge? Find a depressed PhD

Every finite thing fails the infinite test.

Why? Because you're made in God's image. You have God-sized appetites. Nothing God-sized satisfies you except God.

It's like trying to fill the ocean with a garden hose. The ocean won't complain, but it won't be filled.

Your soul is ocean-sized. You keep trying to fill it with garden-hose experiences.

Jesus offers the ocean itself. Not more water. The source of all water.

Not better experiences. The source of all experience.

Not improved meaning. The source of all meaning.

Michael discovered what everyone discovers who's honest: Only the infinite can satisfy the infinite hunger inside you.

And there's only one infinite Person available.

Everything else is finite.

Everyone else is created.

Every other "god" is imaginary.

That's not exclusive because Christians are mean.

That's exclusive because math is true.

THE QUESTION That Ends All Questions

Forget philosophy for a second. It all comes down to one question:

What do you do with Jesus?

C.S. Lewis put it simply: Jesus claimed to be God. That makes Him either:

1 **Liar** (He knew it was false)

2 **Lunatic** (He believed it but was crazy)

3 **Lord** (He was telling the truth)

"Good teacher" isn't an option. Good teachers don't claim to be God unless they're crazy or lying.

Let's check:

Was He lying?

Liars don't usually:

- Live perfect moral lives
- Teach others to be honest
- Die for their lies
- Inspire followers to die for those lies
- Transform the world with fictional stories

Liars lie for gain. Jesus gained crucifixion.

Was He crazy?

Insane people don't usually:

- Give the most quoted wisdom in history
- Stay calm under pressure
- Outmaneuver their critics intellectually
- Build movements that last 2,000 years
- Transform billions of lives positively

Crazy people say crazy things consistently. Jesus said profound things consistently.

Was He Lord?

This explains:

- Why His claims didn't sound crazy to Him (they were true)
- Why He didn't back down when threatened (truth doesn't compromise)
- Why He willingly died (love sacrifices for others)
- Why His followers died for Him (they saw Him alive again)
- Why people still follow Him (He keeps changing lives)

The evidence points to LORD.

But here's the thing: Even if you disagree with the

evidence, you can't ignore the question. Jesus forces everyone to decide:

Is He who He claimed to be?
Because if He is, then He's the only way to God.
If He isn't, then Christianity is the world's biggest lie.
There's no middle ground.
No "Jesus was a good teacher but not God."
No "All religions are basically the same."
No "It doesn't matter what you believe."

It matters. Because if Jesus is Lord, then everyone who ignores Him is missing the whole point of existence.

And if Jesus isn't Lord, then everyone who follows Him is wasting their life on a lie.

The stakes couldn't be higher.
The question couldn't be clearer.
The choice couldn't be more important.
What do YOU do with Jesus?

The Decision Before You

I've told you my story. The boy who took apart stereos, searching for the source of voices. The teenager who tested every religion. The young man who found God in Genesis. The adult who discovered that only Christ satisfies.

Now it's your turn to decide.

The Evidence You've Seen:

- Curiosity that points beyond survival
- Moral conscience that speaks universally
- Success that leaves you empty
- Scripture that reads you while you read it
- Transformation that others notice first
- Faith that sustains through every life stage

- Only one religion that actually delivers what it promises

The Invitation That Stands:

Jesus says, "Come to me, all who labor and are heavy laden, and I will give you rest" (Matthew 11:28).

Not "Try harder."

Not "Be better."

Not "Earn it."

Come. That's it. Come as you are. Bring your questions, doubts, failures, emptiness, searching, and rebellion. He's not surprised by any of it.

The Response Required:

You can't stay neutral on Jesus. Neutral IS a choice. It's choosing to ignore Him.

You can:

1 **Accept** Him as Lord and Savior

2 **Reject** Him as liar or lunatic

3 **Postpone** the decision (which is really rejection)

But you can't say He doesn't matter.

If He's who He claimed to be, He matters more than anything.

If He's not, then nothing ultimately matters.

Either way, the question demands an answer.

What Will You Choose?

The boy with the screwdriver found what he was looking for: The Voice behind all the voices. The Singer behind all the songs. The Meaning behind all the searching.

His name is Jesus.

The only Way.

The only Truth.

The only Life.

And He's been looking for you longer than you've been looking for Him.

The search can end today. Not because you stop asking questions, but because you find the Answer that makes all questions meaningful.

What's it going to be?

---

[1] CORRIE TEN BOOM, *The Hiding Place* (Grand Rapids: Chosen Books, 2006), 217.

ACKNOWLEDGMENTS

Every book is a community effort, even when only one name appears on the cover. This memoir exists because of the faithful people God placed in my life—those who shaped the story, believed in its telling, and supported its creation.

First and always, my wife Lilya—you are the pillar of this project and the foundation of our home. When I hesitated, wondering if my story mattered, you consistently reminded me: "You need to write this book for your kids." Your unwavering support, your belief in the message, and your patience through countless hours of writing made this possible. You saw the book before I did, and you never let me forget why it needed to exist. This book is as much yours as mine.

To my parents—Dad, who slipped into our rooms at 4 AM, praying over each sleeping child by name, planting seeds of faith in the darkness that would bloom in God's perfect time. Mom, whose quiet strength and faithful love provided the foundation for all our seeking. Your prayers and example taught me that faith isn't just believed but lived.

To my brothers—Eduard, Sergey, and Vadim—who have modeled Christ for me in ways words cannot capture. Your lives have been living sermons, your faith a compass when mine wavered. Vadim, that mission trip you signed me up for without asking changed more than you know. Each of you has shown me different facets of following Jesus, and I'm grateful God gave me brothers who became friends and mentors.

To my sisters—Svetlana and Shana. Svetlana, thank you for your prayers and encouragement throughout this journey. Shana, your careful reading and honest feedback shaped every chapter. You helped me find my voice when it felt lost in the details, and your encouragement kept me moving forward when the work felt overwhelming. Thank you both for believing in this story.

To Dr. Timothy Dresselhaus, MD, MPH—your book *Seven Deadly Lies* sparked the fire that became this memoir. Thank you for our deep fellowship, for challenging me to write this story, and for your careful proofreading and theological guidance throughout. Your wisdom and friendship have been gifts from God.

To Dr. Robert Menzies—thank you for your proofreading, theological insights, and encouragement to tell this story with both boldness and grace. Your scholarship and heart for truth strengthened this work immeasurably.

To those who helped choose this book's visual presentation—your input shaped how this story would first meet its readers. Special thanks to my wife Lilya and daughter Naomi for leading this effort, and to Eva Golub, Irina Matveyev, Lori Matveyev, Lana Matveyev, Ruvim & Tanya Yaremkiv, Eliana Natekin, Antonina Sidlinskaya, Emily Sinkin, Rachel Natekin, and Isabelle Matveyev. Your collective wisdom helped select a cover that invites seekers to open these pages and discover the Voice within.

To the countless others who have shaped my journey—friends, mentors, teachers, pastors, and fellow seekers whose names would fill another book—I am deeply grateful. Every conversation, every challenge, every encouragement has been a thread in the tapestry of this story. If you pick up this book and remember our paths crossing, know that you helped write these pages through the impact you had on my life. You are part of this testimony, and I thank God for each of you.

To the curious, the broken, and the seeking who will read these pages—you were in my heart with every word I wrote. My prayer is that you will find in this imperfect story a perfect Savior who has been calling your name all along. May your questions lead you home, just as mine did.

This work benefited from AI-assisted editing for clarity and expression.

All glory to the One who takes broken stories and makes them beautiful, who uses cracked vessels to carry living water, and who transforms curious children into confident believers. Every good thing in this book points to Him; every flaw is mine alone.

Soli Deo Gloria—To God Alone Be Glory

"But we have this treasure in jars of clay, to show that the surpassing power belongs to God and not to us" (2 Corinthians 4:7, ESV).

ABOUT THE AUTHOR

Paul Natekin brings a unique Soviet immigrant perspective to Christian apologetics and international missions. His spiritual memoir chronicles the journey from dismantling stereos as a curious child to discovering authentic faith in Christ through years of searching and questioning. Seminary graduate, Paul co-founded RadioMv/u-Turn Ministry and serves as Chief Editor of "Peace to Your Home" magazine. He specializes in helping skeptics find solid ground for faith while equipping believers to defend Christianity with grace and truth.

paulnatekin.com @paul_nate

www.ingramcontent.com/pod-product-compliance
Lightning Source LLC
Chambersburg PA
CBHW020928090426
42736CB00010B/1074